From
HIRE
to
INSPIRE

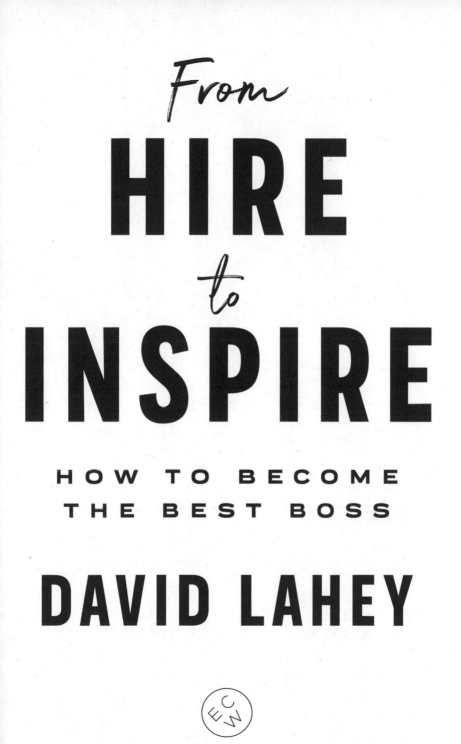

From
HIRE
to
INSPIRE

HOW TO BECOME
THE BEST BOSS

DAVID LAHEY

ECW

Published by ECW Press
665 Gerrard Street East
Toronto, Ontario, Canada M4M 1Y2
416-694-3348 / info@ecwpress.com

Cover design: Michel Vrana
Author photo: Stan Behal

With all terminations, the leader would be wise to obtain the advice of legal council. The author assumes no liability for our statements about terminations.

LIBRARY AND ARCHIVES CANADA CATALOGUING IN PUBLICATION

Title: From hire to inspire : how to become the best boss / David Lahey.

Names: Lahey, David, author.

Identifiers: Canadiana (print) 20190232463
Canadiana (ebook) 20190232471

ISBN 978-1-77041-487-7 (hardcover)
ISBN 978-1-77305-534-3 (PDF)
ISBN 978-1-77305-533-6 (epub)

Subjects: LCSH: Personnel management.
LCSH: Psychology, Industrial.

Classification: LCC HF5549 .L34 2020
DDC 658.3—dc23

The publication of *From Hire to Inspire* has been funded in part by the Government of Canada. *Ce livre est financé en partie par le gouvernement du Canada.* We also acknowledge the contribution of the Government of Ontario through the Ontario Book Publishing Tax Credit, and through Ontario Creates for the marketing of this book.

PRINTED AND BOUND IN CANADA

PRINTING: FRIESENS 5 4 3 2 1

This book is dedicated to my wife, Patty.
Beautiful, smart, edgy, persuasive and fun.
My best boss leader, you make me a better person.

Table of Contents

Acknowledgments

I would like to thank several people for their support and input in the creation of this book.

My publisher, Jack David from ECW Press, kept me moving along and was most helpful in the process, timing and delivery. Jack, thank you. To my team at Predictive Success and all the wonderful clients we have worked with across North America, thank you. Thank you for the trust of allowing me to consult and work with your dreams and business goals.

To my business partners at the Predictive Index LLC, www.predictiveindex.com, Mike Zani and Daniel Muzquiz. These two visionary software leaders are creating a new category, Talent Optimization, www.talentoptimization.org, which will unleash new levels of productivity for leaders everywhere. Both of you and your company create a better work and better world environments for thousands of organizations globally each and every day. Thank you.

Lastly, to my first "bosses," my departed mother, Shirley, and father, Orville. You both just cared, supported, challenged, nurtured and celebrated with me. Your impact has lasted all these decades later. I can only pay it forward to thank you.

Chapter 1

Getting to "Best Boss" Status

"The best leader is the one who has sense enough to pick good men to do what he wants done, and the self-restraint to keep from meddling with them while they do it."

— THEODORE ROOSEVELT

Many of us will finish our lives having worked for 90,000 hours — a third of our turn on this planet. More alarming: many of us will spend those working hours at jobs we hate under the supervision of bosses whose power to inspire is lacking. What a shame. We work in order to buy things and enjoy experiences and fill our lives with pleasure and comfort. Such aspirations are critical to creating a better existence for those who aspire to live in North America. Having a job you love and a boss you like is key to making this 90,000-hour investment a fruitful one. My life has included lots of fruit. In fact, I had one job, as an enterprise manager at Microsoft, that was such a thrill that I never knew when quitting time was, seldom watched for long weekends and was quoted as saying I would "take two bullets" for my boss. This was nirvana: a job that suited my personality and a boss — Randy Lenaghan — who allowed me to just do it. Randy was a mindful boss, aware of the buttons to push with his employees, a "Chief Talent Optimizer" of the talent of his team. Pure joy.

Connecting business strategy to business results

Randy understood that well-run business units and companies have a business strategy that's linked to an expectation of nominated business results. He knew what we all need to know: that to be successful, companies need to acknowledge that people are at their heart, and that leaders need to understand the piece about aligning them with a business strategy. This is the journey to Talent Optimization, and everyone should take it: www. talentoptimization.org.

A business can create key success criteria, but at the end of the fiscal year, the determination of success relies on whether the people in the business performed. The most successful companies are the ones that were able to put the best people in the right positions.

Rewinding back to the beginning of the fiscal year, that same business will have set out to develop a strategic plan that can set them up for these successes. The sweet spot, then, is in that region between the business strategy and the business results. How do companies ensure they are setting themselves up for success?

Talent optimization is a four-part discipline that gives companies the ability to diagnose their business, design their strategy, hire the right fits for jobs and inspire these individuals to stay and grow with the company.

People must be aligned with the business strategy in order for the company to achieve its goals by year end.

Talent optimization isn't about developing a new business strategy. We like the way the Boston software firm, the

Predictive Index LLC, has laid it out below. What gets in the way of a leader's business results is its lacking of three essentials: a proper diagnosis for job models, an appreciation for hiring with purpose and the best possible data to inspire employees to crush the business results. The people section often gets ignored and this hampers leaders and business units' chances of beating their numbers.

The world today — awash in jobs but without enough people to fill them — is in an envious spot. Or at least it might seem that way at first blush. In point of fact, the scene is a frustrating one for managers, whose ongoing pursuit of players sees them in constant hiring mode, forever chasing workers willing to hang around long enough to make all the effort worthwhile.

Here's where the concept of talent optimization earns its stripes as a game changer.

Talent optimization is the link between a company's business strategy — higher quotas, increased sales, more good done, less pain caused, fewer risks taken — and the end result it seeks, say, twelve months later — lower risks, fewer accidents, decreased operational costs, higher revenues. It is the magic in the middle of these points, and it begins with taking an intentional and data-driven approach to getting the people part right.

As a business leader, it's your job to ensure that your company puts your talent into an optimal position for producing desired business results and besting the competition. Talent optimization is the relatively new term that exploits the relatively old considerations of people, process and technology and uncovers the connection between business strategy and its results. It's a different way to understand how people fit into a broader business plan and to optimize output and productivity to achieve impressive results. In this bridge between strategy and outcome, this process facilitates designing jobs with purpose and then hiring for them in an agreed-upon and — because your managers are helping you create the models — consistent way.

Talent optimization also protects against employee disengagement, the scourge of the productive office. This widespread issue (by some measures, more than 70 percent of employees in the US are disengaged), whose hallmarks are poor productivity, absenteeism, poor client service and toxic workplace cultures, deprives organizations of billions of dollars.

At a certain point, every manager needs to appreciate that there's a better approach to staffing their ranks than what they've taken up to now, that they can't just keep hiring this person and that, posting jobs on Indeed, giving somebody's golf buddy or squash pal a try. On the one side of the equation, there's no question that managers have biases. And on the other, there's no question that jobs still need to be filled according to skills and will. So what's missing? The proper job models. An analytic process that's predictive and prescriptive and that maps jobs for the best chances of success. And a way to design them so they're mindful of external pressures, like having to hire someone by year end to get a bonus. Indeed, these are the things most likely to make a boss steamroll over whatever model they had in place, just to jump from business strategy to results and skip the middle parts. It's one of the things I see that frustrates me the most.

It's worth noting, too, that people in HR (for the most part) have not been professionally trained to undertake these tasks. Human resource professionals have non-analytical backgrounds, and don't understand the finer points of job models. Sure, if you go into a lean Six Sigma company, they know how to do this, they have specialists who understand the details. But it's too expensive for most companies to hire a chief analytic officer, though that's a trend we're seeing among the Fortune 500.

So talent optimization means we yoga breath this and we say, Let's design a job that maps to where we want to go as an organization. This applies to for-profit and social profit organization. Where we want our sales to be, our finance, our costs, etc. Let's use an analytic approach also to look at our top performers, to compare the inside success people experience to the job model of their purported role, almost like a sound check. And then let's hire to that model so we can diagnose misfits, so we can high-five good selections.

Most businesses have some kind of business strategy. Those companies without a strategy most often fade away or are not serious in their mission. Often this strategy all too often reads out in technical or functional terms, and the people part is missing or disconnected. Talent optimization provides context that will inform an analytic approach that offers up diagnosed data on how to onboard, coach and mentor individuals — and all from *their* world, not the one the boss lives in. Importantly, talent optimization does not advocate the creation of a new business strategy. It's about translating your existing specific, documented and actionable one into sought-after business results through a human lens.

When companies are examining this concept, they'll often start with zero — we call it level zero: no objective data to hire. Here is the age-old practice of hiring by gut, our *golden gut.* But as Robert Frost famously warned, nothing gold can stay. There's no formal engagement survey with this approach, there's no performance, no analytics. It's simply: I like you, so I'll hire you. That's not enough. You need to measure what matters, analyze the evidence and prescribe actions to improve things. Anything else is just spinning your wheels.

The first stage is diagnosis, which means surveying all employees to see who's who in the zoo so you know what you're working with. Just as a doctor considers symptoms, context, possible explanations, a talent optimizer identifies potential issues that might be at the root of a workplace challenge in pursuit of a more productive and engaged workforce.

The first days of diagnosis are the most important. We may have the wrong people in the wrong seats, and taking stock of our stash responsively is key. Instead of letting problems build up and fester, prompt attention shows employees we care. Otherwise, it would be like going in to buy a car and the sales guy not asking you if you want a convertible or an S series Mercedes, without knowing if you have a family, what your budget is, your tastes, just selling you the next vehicle that comes up. It's a truly reckless approach.

And yet we do it at work and it's the number-one cost companies bear.

Level one is where we start to collect basic data, maybe do a Myers–Briggs on the whole crew of staffers, maybe figure out their colors. Executive might get sent here to an industrial organizational psychologist. Some companies will spend $4k on senior people before they hire them. So while an organization might say they're addressing level one, they're doing so inconsistently.

Level two is all about job design. Here, we're talking about a prescriptive model with a wee bit of research that allows us to survey important and recurring aspects of a job in order to best set a person up for success in that role. Maybe the job calls for a certain level of extraversion or assertiveness, speed or patience, attention to formality or detail. The job design might include a call for cognitive agility — how fast the person filling it would need to calibrate conversations. Maybe it has requirements around decision-making, flexibility, EQ and congruency.

Here is where science meets flesh and blood — and companies would do well to pay attention. Too often they'll merely take a nibble of analytics, maybe spring for a team-building event and then put away its results never to be seen again. Maybe they explore colors, and discover that she's a red and he's a blue. Or I'm an INTG and the guy down the hall is an ESTP. But none of this sticks or is memorable. It doesn't get used outside of that half-day team event, and it doesn't live and breathe in the corporate lungs.

The third piece is having a purposeful way to hire that is thoughtful, that understands the business strategy, that has drawn a line from it to results. This is the part that appreciates the people piece, that acknowledges that it is the most expensive thing on the balance sheet. Here, every employee is surveyed and subject to an analytic view of their DNA. It's an extensive, rigorous procedure that is, at last, all about compassion. The best leaders care about the candidates and know that, when they've been set up for success and are matched with jobs whose designs correspond with their core DNA, they'll be happier, more engaged and more inclined to hang around.

Level three really is about the company's ability to analyze the full organizational map in the journey from business strategy to business results, and it's seen through predictive analytics to which all team members have access. The data is current and consistently mapped to the business plan.

Very few companies are at level three. Leaders of better companies understand that it's in their best interest to look at a different way of understanding their culture, predicting where they need to go, architecting the teams of the future and creating an aligned path from business strategy to business results that is transparent, reinforced and predictable. When I was at Microsoft in the 1990s, they had great software but no enterprise teams. So they had very poor relationships with banks. My team was hired to cultivate these critical relationships and to do it strategically versus tactically — i.e., just selling software boxes. At that point, Microsoft hired people with strong technical skills, full stop. They had no analytics approach to hiring managers with people skills. Microsoft in the 1990s could be summed up with the following: high technical vision, low people vision.

Today, a level-three company would be an organization like Google. They have a people analytics team, they measure everything, and they have equipped their leaders with very strong analytics. These are the companies that bring a cognitive agility approach to measuring potential and trainability and time to success in a role.

We hire a lot of millennials at Predictive Success, and we know the average millennial stays with a job for only about 2.1 years. But if I'm able to map their world to my world with a job design, I can get them up to four years. And if I can get them to four years, I just might be able to get them to six or seven. Having diagnosed a purposeful process for hiring this soul, you now have them by the hand and can ask yourself, How do I use that same data and insight for inspiration so I can keep them engaged? Gallup says as many as 50 percent of your employees are disengaged; GlassDoor says 47 percent of new employees believe they could find another job in six months at any time. These points of pressure force us to embrace any insight that might keep an employee with us longer.

So inspiration is the last piece of the talent-optimization puzzle. It's the follow-up that recognizes that getting folks to sign on and feel valuable is one thing; keeping them jazzed is another. Once you've hired with purpose and created a great job design benchmarked against the best in the sector, it's important next to train frontline supervisors to be analytically aware so they can spot the best path for employees working beneath them and can treat them according to their world. The supervisor can consider things like rewards and recognition, how they like to be celebrated, preparation for performance reviews and how to best deliver them with impact. And they, this baseline of managers who care about hiring and developing their employees and teams, can set themselves up to create the next level of managers one, three, five, seven years down the road.

Talent optimization is a deliberate, purposeful process that allows a company to compete for talent, deliver on its mission, leverage its internal assets and be a better operator of people. The focus is quite narrow, and it has to be. Otherwise, there are too many distractions. Everybody's in meetings all day long, wanting to do the right thing but too diverted by outside business to ensure it. It's simply too risky to just bring in another set of arms and legs and see what happens. It's bad for the brand, bad for your GlassDoor ratings, bad for your continuance. This strategy, like all strategies, needs to be actionable.

That distinction is key. Sometimes people will hire a Deloitte or a McKinsey to come in and give them a grandiose strategy, then they leave after paying the bill and never see it through. Better to have a wander over to www.talentoptimization.org, where there's all kinds of explanations and best practices and plans for action.

Key, too, is that the talent-optimization efforts are owned by everyone: the HR business partners, the executive, the CEO, the frontline supervisor, external partners. Talent optimization must be embraced by leaders at every level. Though it's got to begin with buy-in at the top, and execs are its champions, it won't work if it's only implemented in the C-suite. The fundamental base in all of this is to "unlock" the discretionary effort of each and every employee.

Discretionary effort

There's too much risk associated with bringing someone into a job who isn't a good fit for it. This is where the idea of discretionary effort needs attention. Normal people just want to go to a job that fits them. And why not? A job that fits you leaves you happier, more engaged, laboring away happily, without one eye on the clock. But people in roles that aren't a match for their personality become what I call chair spinners. This is someone who doesn't like their job, who, at 5:01, springs from their chair for the train station so fast that it doesn't stop spinning till they come back the next morning. We call the great gulf between the chair spinners and the people who genuinely love their work discretionary effort.

Disengagement causes employees to withhold discretionary effort and to only deliver the bare minimum of work to stay employed. Proponents of talent optimization have nominated four factors that cause disengagement:

- Misalignment with the job: Poorly defined positions, sloppy hiring processes or evolving business needs create a mismatch between employees and their roles. Lack of job fit directly impacts motivation and productivity.
- Misalignment with the manager: The relationship between employees and their managers is the most critical contributor to engagement, yet many managers are poorly equipped or not trained to effectively understand their employees' individual needs. They struggle to communicate with and motivate their employees.
- Misalignment with the team: Team-based work is more critical than ever, yet poor communication, insufficient collaboration and inability to manage the tensions inherent to teamwork continue to extract a massive tax on productivity and innovation.
- Misalignment with culture: To be productive and engaged, employees need to feel they belong. When they feel out of tune with their organization's values, or when they lose trust in their leadership, their own performance suffers, and they can create a toxic work environment that undermines productivity.

When a job has been designed with purpose, when the dimensions and particulars of the person going into it have been well studied, when the employees have been properly coached for a strong culture of trust and cultural championship-building, everyone — the employee, the manager, the team — and the culture are stronger. There's more work getting done, there's more pleasure in the doing. It's not about having stand-up desks and cool perks at the office. That is a silly way to motivate your staff to gain discretionary success. Study the analytics and understand what you're looking for in the creation of the job. Create the job with purpose, hire that person and cradle them from hire to inspire.

We're measuring what matters, we're going to track it, really analyze the evidence. Every year, we should be studying who our top performers were, who had the highest reviews, who showed up for more events, which group had the highest engagement. We should be singling out whether the company culture is out of vogue with today's business cycle, if there are poor senior dynamics at the top of the house. We should be identifying the areas of the company that are flagging and figuring out who those areas' leaders are. Consider: do these people need to be promoted to customers?

One thing that's for sure is that, in this war for talent, if we don't do something, we're going to keep getting what we're getting. If we don't equip our leaders to be better with talent, to employ new insights to the finding, keeping and inspiring of their employees, we're going to lose this war.

Talent optimization in action

Recently, Predictive Success was hired to work with a company called BlackBerry. After we had a meeting with their head of sales and HR leader in the UK, we approached our millennial shared-services team and were dismayed to learn that they didn't even know who BlackBerry was. This is a great example of a Canadian icon who had great technology but no predictable model for creating a dynamic sales team. And now here they are in 2019 — a software company today, versus an appliance company — with a strategy to go and sell to enterprise clients. They have wonderful software that's used by the biggest governments in the world. But they need to spread the word.

Where they're trying to move to is the design of an enterprise strategy that would allow them to hire salespeople capable of establishing new relationships, new trust with a brand that many people thought was gone and now is as strong as it's ever been in the security part of the communication process in banks and governments, protecting companies from exposure, networking problems and security issues. We've just started to create a job model in their UK offices to help them predict those enterprise salespeople who can circulate and cultivate the great relationships that will bring them business and elevate the brand. We are mapping the software and technical prowess of BlackBerry to the strategies of CEOs in banks and government agencies, designing with purpose, hiring to job models and providing new insight to the sales managers in a very lean way because cost is a real concern. This will be an interesting process to follow.

30K is a software company based in San Francisco with an API that works with travel companies like Kayak and Expedia to allow customers to understand what's included in their flight. As well, the company partners with airlines to provide better rewards service, and to reap the loyalty of their returning customers. This growing company knew hiring had to be efficient and productive if they were to ride the wave to success. Talent optimization allowed leaders to narrow down a large stack of resumes and only spend time on those whose behavioral profiles fit the job model. In the last round of hires, 30k received 102 applications for five jobs. After sending behavioral and cognitive assessments to the most promising candidates, the company was able to narrow the potentials list down to the eight they wanted to interview. Before adopting this more focused approach, this number would've been thirty to forty.

Importantly, ten months after the hires joined the team, they talked about loving their jobs and were visibly glowing at work. By hiring based on the behavioral and cognitive assessments, 30k was able to hire cultural champions with the right characteristics for the job and attitudes for growth.

Recently, Canadians were surprised to find themselves living in a hotbed for basketball. The Toronto Raptors powered through their 2019 season and, with an NBA championship at the end, drew to a close the team's twenty-four-year association with misses. Today, the business strategy was not only to make money but to win a championship. Process saw that through, ushered into the vacuum by coach Nick Nurse. He understood that all the players (not just the superstars) have a role to play. Even the castoffs and has-beens. Nurse matched the player to the job design and was able to use a different approach to inspire everyone. The results were phenomenal.

The thing with Nurse is that he appreciated that he had to create a team in order to coach it. He's a very smart leader, an example of someone who understands the value of talent optimization — and of applying its lessons to a changing sport that's elevated three-pointers from the corner to massive proportions. He designed his entire training camp around this new set of rules. In his practices, three-pointers counted for four points. What that job design did was map the probability of winning an NBA championship to a team's ability to shoot three-pointers. He was able to change the job design and recognize this evolving piece of training. The result was a substantial change in results. Basketball now is a three-point gambit. Talent optimization wins the game.

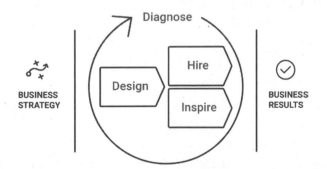

Source: the Predictive Index®, a registered trademark of Predictive Index LLC and used here with permission.

Talent optimization is about translating an organization's well-designed strategy into business results through a human lens. Predictive analytics can help. This discipline is all about assisting leaders to create purposeful job models and to place the right people into the right roles.

Finding a job that delights you is one of your life's most fundamental tasks. If you can't do that, you can't be any good to anyone else around you. This maxim is a favorite, hauled out as support in aid of a range of applications. I'm talking about the flight-emergency concept, in which adults are urged to negotiate their own oxygen masks before turning their attention to anyone else. The same wisdom extends to the workplace and the attention managers need pay to their own state before imagining they can effect any impact on their staffers.

Why do some people just excel as the boss? Working with hundreds of companies across North America, I have seen some darn good leaders, and some leaders that should be "promoted to happy alumni," as my friend Mike Zani, CEO of the Predictive Index, calls it. A good boss can have an enormous impact on the employees in his oversight. He can influence their happiness, their success, their life. Employees want a lot of things, but the real juice they seek is simple predictability from their immediate boss. Why would any employee not want to have a great boss who truly understands their drives and behaviors at work? Often, that bad boss is simply a person who isn't in the right role. Or who has the wrong insights on his employees or doesn't know how to relate to them. Either way, it's a risk. We know that people leave bosses.

In over twenty-five years of working with some leaders who were rock solid and others who were mushy weak, I noticed that many managers don't know enough about what kind of work their people enjoy. Unfortunately, it is only when a company performs exit interviews that this kind of information comes out. In many companies, this has been a routine practice; the HR department finds out why talented people are leaving and what would have convinced them to stick around. With unemployment rates at historic lows, this approach misses the boat.

I worked with some very innovative leaders at Microsoft in Redmond and Toronto — leaders I would call strong in vision and weak in people skills. There was Randy at Microsoft, whom I would've defended from gunplay. And there were others, with whom it's just as well there were no guns to be had. Randy Lenaghan created a culture in which his team members were all self-aware and each was managed from their own world, and we excelled. Sales targets were constantly exceeded. We made tons of money, we were graciously included in the distribution of share options each year and we were happy.

I worked with a large, 55,000-employee bank whose CIO was appointed by the CEO and given absolute control to clean up an IT team led by a former IBM executive. Talk about being in tight with a supplier pulling the people strings!

My father was an entrepreneur. He ran a manufacturing company that made large industrial brushes for street sweepers. The company was agile, with only a few "hands dirty"-type leaders. It made money and attracted new employees with its culture. My dad created a small pool of cultural champion leaders — he was way ahead of his time. The employees loved working for him and were engaged, and my dad truly avoided keeping "silent killer" employees who would take your money but still be disengaged at work.

Is your boss the worst part of your job?

Three out of four employees report that their boss is the worst and most stressful part of their job. It's simply not cool that most people work hard to obtain a degree in something they're passionate about, that they put the energy and toil into creating a professional life that pleases them, and that they then have to deal with some knucklehead who can't lead properly.

In a perfect world, managers care about their workers. They oversee a workplace where all employees are equals, and they work alongside them, cultivating inspiring opportunities for them to excel and grow. This is the world of the mindful boss. This is the path to the best boss.

Mindfulness is hardly a new concept. Indeed, the phrase made the journey from new-age fringedom to mainstream de rigueur like a bullet. Not so swiftly accepted, however, has been the idea that managers need to adopt the mindfulness outlook not only to their own lives but to their oversight of employees. In other words, it's important for leaders to become more present, aware and purposeful in their personal behavior, yes, but it's just as important that they draw from the same well in their dealings with their professional subordinates. When the circle is complete, the entire organization benefits.

In my work with over 500 leading companies across North America, I've recognized abundantly that the truly successful companies are the ones whose leaders are in the "mindful mindset." These are the leaders who apply this thoughtful strategy to all their relationships. We have seen this enhance the work-life balance when managers are mindful of those whose presence they're in. Mindfulness can be defined as moment-by-moment awareness of your thoughts, feelings, bodily sensations and surrounding environment. When you are mindful, you accept. You give attention to thoughts and feelings without judging whether they are right or wrong. You are present, you are aware, you bring all analytics to help you manage people and change. The "best boss" looks for all advantages to engage, inspire and grow, and for tools to help with decisions.

The mindful leader is laser-focused and in the awareness zone. She knows that multitasking is the enemy of mindful focus. Social media and "always-on" technology enable many of us to spend our days in a state of divided attention and near-constant multitasking. This keeps us from truly living in the present. Studies have found that when people are interrupted and divide their attention, it takes them 50 percent longer to accomplish a task, and they're 50 percent likelier to make errors. Smart leaders read people, not devices. I have never seen an iPhone understand an employee who is having a personal problem or needs a new approach to address a presentation with a grumpy executive.

How is a "best boss" created?

How does someone get to "best boss" status? It is tied closely to being a mindful manager, which makes you a selfless leader. The mindful leader is not focused on herself. The mindful leader understands that the story about her is a story that includes other people. Effective leadership, after all, is the effective embodiment of others.

I believe the best leader is always looking for a new angle, a new edge of insight on how to get her team to the next level. We all have access to the one-day "pump" courses, the two-day retreats and even the one-week Executive MBA from McGill. When we look to bring in new data to the frontline leader — new predictive and prescriptive analytics on who she should hire, how she should onboard the newbie and how she can keep that employee — we get an accelerator that will make her job way easier. I have seen dramatic success when a leader is trained as an analyst in the use of predictive analytics like the Predictive Index software. The new "people radar" concept of having objective data on the core drives and behaviors of the employee is always welcome. In the old days, assessments were perhaps done once and kept in some dark, hidden HR or personnel folder. What a total waste. A best boss wants this data and to be trained in using it to best effect. With the unemployment rates in America at their lowest levels in forty-nine years, your employees have too many options for leaving you. If you are not in their "world," managing them uniquely and objectively, they will bolt to another company. The quit rate is up across all states by an average of 13 to 20 percent.

How a leader approaches the task of managing other souls plays significantly into how willingly they respond, and, in turn, how successfully the enterprise as a whole operates.

Each leader comes from a past. She might have grown up a middle child, or the eldest or the youngest. She might have gotten married or divorced. She might have travelled or stuck close to home. She might have earned a double PhD or be self-taught. Each leader has a background of some level of education, personal connection, family experience; each leader has a personal history of success. Acknowledging and understanding these points of difference is not only inevitable but critical. After all, it is only by appreciating her particular patterns and approaches to management that a leader can capitalize on them. If we can home in on those channels that facilitate the most effective communication with others because they tune in most applicably to the characteristics that mark our genuine selves, we'll enjoy the most success.

I have seen that all employees learn about new skills and processes at different paces. Not all of your employees will have the same cognitive "agility." Why is it then that companies and leaders train all employees at the same speed? A guaranteed route to failure. Leading companies that insert cognitive assessment/analytics create a new runway to learning. If a leader has data on who on his team needs a much longer runway to learn new concepts and who learns with a short takeoff and landing approach, he will be more efficient in his messaging and more successful with his teams.

Software is the enabler here. From work I have done back at Microsoft, I remember that some very smart people have very low cognitive agility. If you tried to move too fast with new concepts with these people, they would revolt, and your training would be a disaster. I once hired Eugene Piric, a very smart, energetic Serbian with a thick accent who was new to Canada. We could not validate Eugene's engineering degree as his country was at war during our hiring. However, Eugene had a very high cognitive score. We took the risk and hired him, and he was a quick read, a dramatic success and one of the top enterprise strategic consultants in Microsoft. He is now country manager back in Serbia. This is all due to the insight and attention I paid to predictive analytics and potential.

The new journey to "Chief Talent Optimizer"

The reality over the next long stretch of corporate evolution is that success will massively tie in to the supply and demand of talent. The war for talent is over, and talent won. In other words, the baby boomers are retiring and increasingly shifting their physical presence onto the golf courses. Worryingly, there aren't as many people around to backfill their posts as are required. And the manager who's not pushing the right buttons will have a tougher time recruiting and retaining people than the manager who's pushing the right ones.

The employees coming into the market will have ten to twelve jobs in their career. They will have many more choices than perhaps any other generation. They will also have a new level of power, since they can leave a bad boss very easily. Earlier generations had fewer choices. They were raised by parents who maybe experienced severe grief and turmoil, the recession or even the Great Depression. They were taught to get that solid job and stay for life. We still see employees who have hung around for thirty, forty or even fifty years at one single employer. The employers back then had a personal covenant with their employees. This was a time before venture capitalists, before pump-and-dump corporate raiders, when loyalty between employee and company was commonplace.

This all changed in the 1990s and 2000s, when companies were being purchased and stripped at record speeds. Finance teams saw great value in breaking up units and selling off the poorer performers or simply reducing headcount and increasing automation. The trust bond was broken; the job-for-life concept had reached a fork in the road. Today's newer candidates grew up through all this. They saw their parents lose jobs, get outsourced, get demoted, get angry. They don't want that. They are looking for an "experience" at work. This has changed how the boss/leader must lead. She is becoming the experience creator.

We know that for a boss/leader to get even close to "commitment" from the millennial group of employees, a fresh approach is needed. You must develop predictive skills and design a process to hire purposely. You must inspire effectively and measure and self-diagnose — often on the fly — how you handle your talent. It is a race to establish yourself as a leader of your talent. The new C-level role of your team in the years ahead really will be as "Chief Talent Optimizer." As with all C-level roles, you will need as much data and predictability as you can get to run the business.

Studying the ever-present millennials, we can see that they cherish experiences as probably their number-one drive in life. I have three millennial children. When my wife, Patty, and I offer them a neat experience, they are all in. If this group buys into your vision, and more importantly your "cause," you will get them to almost become workaholics.

A recent study by Harris Poll (for Eventbrite) showed that 78 percent of millennials would rather spend money on an experience than a material purchase. Best boss leaders would be wise to leverage this data for their rewards and recognition programs.

According to a 2018 Deloitte report, approximately 43 percent of millennials envision leaving their jobs within two years. Scarier still for leaders is the news that only 28 percent seek to stay beyond five years. Best boss leaders need to know that this new group will actually leave and would be wise to add in unique training "experiences" to help keep them for even one or two additional years. Don't count on many staying ten to fifteen years here.

And as we look forward, we see there's a new generation entering the workforce. They're the frontlines of Gen Z (those born between 1995 and 2010), and they mark the entrance of a new breed of workers. Employed GenZ respondents express even less loyalty than their predecessors, with 61 percent saying they would leave within two years if given the choice. The bosses today have to manage several generations, all with unique values. Predictive analytics provides real data on each person from any generation. I like to call it a "radar detector" on who is going too fast for their current role and who will get bored there.

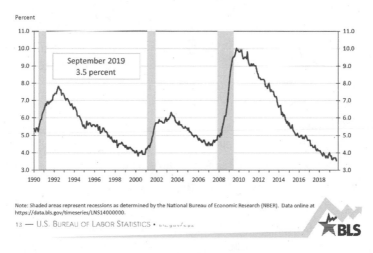

Chart 10. Civilian unemployment rate
Seasonally adjusted, 1990–2019

Source: US Bureau of Statistics, www.bls.gov/web/empsit/cps_charts.pdf

Enter the distinction between the compliance manager and the commitment manager. Where the old-style (i.e., compliance) manager could insist on attendance in his office when told, or decree an employee take his vacation at a time that suited the company, the new-style (i.e., commitment) manager is a different beast. Compliance, for her, is utterly trumped by commitment. And commitment, as the tuned-in leaders know all too well, only comes from engagement.

Gallup writes that 33 percent of your workforce is disengaged. Why is that? That's easy. It's the boss. As I have stated already, people leave their boss, not their company. In 2006, I decided to leave a career at Microsoft to move into analytics. I had seen that McKinsey and other leading consulting companies were presenting new insight about the need for better people analytics in the new quest to increase productivity in the workforce. I had been fortunate enough to have been trained by a Boston company, the Predictive Index, in the use of Predictive Index analytics for hiring, coaching and succession planning while working in the paper business in the 1980s. I contacted the CEO at the time, Dinah Daniels, and set up a meeting.

Dinah was the daughter of the founder of a very cool scientific survey that consisted of only two questions and was very fast to use. It was not one of those forty-five-minute tests used for hiring. I really liked the software — so much that I offered to buy the Canadian operation. I saw the need to bring predictive analytics right to the shop floor, right into the hands of the CEO, the executive team and even the frontline leader/boss team. This was thirteen years ago, and the bet was, I am happy to say, a great one. We caught the rising wave to predictive and prescriptive analytics.

Our research at Predictive Success focuses a lot more time on the bottleneck of quit rates at companies. Increasingly, objective, actionable, predictive data is a great employee engagement tool for the frontline leader. I saw a trend forming back in 2006 that was slowly going to challenge why we hire and how we keep employees. Gone were the old days when HR was the master in the hiring process. They would run the job ad, organize the interview room, book the interviews and shortlist the final candidates. Pressures to fill the role demanded they just "do it" and get the business people fast.

The last decade has brought in tremendous new pressures to get the hiring right. Pressures to hire people who can be future culture champions and won't become contaminants or "silent killers." From my experience, it seemed a much better idea to introduce, at the early stage of the hiring cycle, in alignment with the frontline manager/boss, new predictive analytics (evidence) for hires who would still be with the company ninety days and much longer after the hiring event.

The mindful manager is looking for different success thermostats. She needs different data, different ways of selecting, monitoring, coaching and counselling her employees. That is one of the big reasons we see the growth of psychometric testing (15 percent per year), the popularity of coaching and the leaps-and-bounds increase in the use of analytics. In the past, a personality test, like a Myers–Briggs test, was done once and the results were tucked into a file that, so long as the employee didn't get caught up in a workplace scandal, was never looked at again. Or the executives were sent on one-day leadership retreats at great expense to their firms, and the results were never put to any meaningful use.

Company CEOs get financial data on operating costs, monthly balance sheets, income statements and cash-flow reports — but do they get "people analytic reports" on a regular basis? We see that the CEO is more interested in people data than ever before. Analytics that produce data on who is engaged and that offer models of what he needs to hire to execute on his vision are necessary and add to predictability in success.

Modern managers understand that, if one knows an employee's core DNA and personality, one can engage with them to best effect. It's a revelation that arguably hit the world of sports before the business population tapped into it. One of the best examples can be found in the transformative story of a famous basketball coach at the University of Tennessee, Pat Summitt. Summitt was a compliance leader until one of her boosters, a notable alumnus, told her she was recklessly burning through her student athlete supply by not meaningfully tapping into the attributes each brought to the table. She listened to the advice and shifted her approach from a "broom mentality" to a "groom mentality." She brought in analytics to understand which buttons to push in each of her players and came to realize, for example, that certain of her athletes could not bear to be publicly berated in front of their teammates, whereas others thrived on it. Free throws, an integral part of the game, were revealed in a fresh light through the exercise, with analytics unearthing the new information about the call for a sequential, routine-loving personality for best success. She used all of this data to help her calibrate when and how to deliver her messages, and to strategize the specifics of her coaching intervention. It was thus that a compliance manager evolved into a commitment manager.

Your world vs. mine

The universe is crawling with compliance managers. We can see this in many sectors, though certain government agencies might seem most obvious. You see them in bad restaurants, you see them in retailers. These are the folks who clawed their way to the top on the back of the old system. Utterly convinced of the legitimacy of their professional post, these leaders are all about ego. They worked like dogs (either with real work or by being very political) to get where they are, after all, and now they're going to preside from that lofty post like a boss. If you're a compliance manager, you make all your decisions from *your world*.

Recently at Predictive Success, we had an experience in purchasing new appliances for our office that presented us with issues around service and delivery. In a series of escalations, the president of this Toronto-based company avoided resolution. What tone did this set for his team? Why did he not care about the issue? I wondered how he even got into the role as president. I later found out that the company is a family-run business. Compliance starts at the top. Often, compliance-led leadership occurs when the owners are not listening to their market any longer. They are only focused on maximizing short-term profit. Too bad. The end result with compliance leaders (except in government, though even this is now changing a wee bit) is that it must always be "my way or the highway." This does not work in the long term today.

Recently, as our company expanded, we purchased the old Silverwood Dairy in downtown Whitby, Ontario. During our extensive renovations on this 10,000-square-foot facility, we discovered an old "perch," or loft, in the back of the plant with a "looking window." I could not help but think of those factory-floor workers below the smoke-filled perch where, most likely, an old-school, curmudgeonly leader with a hawk eye was ready to pounce on any non-compliance. I reflect on this sometimes when I am up in our very cool modern loft, now with glass tables, low-back comfy chairs and funky media stands, and the contrast to yesterday and yesterday's compliance boss/leaders is dramatic.

A committed leader has a different point of view. He under-stands that success more likely lies in a strategy that considers the situation of the recipient more than the situation of the provider. Here, a manager pauses to think about the worldview of the person whose buy-in he is working to secure, usefully cognizant of the great quantity of biases each of us has natu-rally built into our psyche. The more data this manager has on the particulars of the other person, the more effectively he can communicate with them.

This subject tracks back, too, to a person's ability to elevate a conversation to a place where it is mindful of its perceived value for the other. Every employee has different values that spring from their personality, drive, upbringing and so on. Often, those values are tied in to what we consider core personality traits: assertiveness, extraversion, technical aptitude, patience, detail orientation and so on. So if you've got a person who values a high level of detail, say, you'd better not look to corner them in a super-casual hallway chat.

Beyond that, consider: Some people are natural readers. The written word is their specialty, and the most predictably successful means of connecting with them has always been through text on a page. Others, however, are more inclined to communicate verbally. For these folks, no message hits home more resoundingly than one delivered by voice. Now, let's say that the manager was of the latter camp and the subordinate she was seeking to influence was of the former. What would likely prove the most successful communication approach for this interaction? (Points for anyone who guessed a lengthy and literate letter of understanding.)

When I was at Microsoft, we used to say that if we had all the people in the right roles, we'd be golfing in June. But if we didn't, we'd spend the month scrambling.

We once did some work with SaskPower, an interesting gig for the riskiness of the jobs in question. Here's where a manager really earns his mettle. These workers might interview very well but have no attention for detail and be very impatient and asser-tive. Then you put them in a bucket truck where they have power, or in a transportation vehicle on the highway. If a manager was trained in analytics and was able to understand the core drives of the people they were hiring, they may not want to put them in positions of physical risk. Our research has proven that if you put people in jobs that are absolutely not suited to their core behavior (you put them in because you like them, but they don't natively have the data or sequence or process to be a long-haul transportation driver, say), there's a risk. And shame on you.

If you had a radar on that type of worker, and could know

that his risk profile was higher than average and the probability of his engaging in risky behavior ramped up, you'd be in a better position. You have founders who are very risk-tolerant, very growth-oriented, have huge energy levels, but who don't know when to turn it off. They're not safe bosses or leaders. We're going to see an emergence of tools and analytics that work like a pressure gauge — wearables for your wrist that tell you when it's time to go to bed and stop doing work. Bill Clinton could benefit from something like this. Here is someone who connects very quickly with others, is very assertive, very collaborative and has a tremendous sense of energy.

I would guess that the Predictive Index analytics for Bill Clinton would show he probably has no detail, no filter to say when to stop — both in his political career and his personal life. He was a leader who was dramatically persuasive, and this was coupled with the tenacity to make risky decisions. His numerous liaisons probably are a result. He has an abnormally high ability to read a room and has a large energy "gas tank" that allowed him to get easily distracted and into deviant activities. His style is one where if you had someone manage it, in today's world, he would've been shut down. He's someone who needed to be controlled. We see boss/leaders in the workplace like Clinton. We love their energy, and would be wise to understand how to best harvest this for positive work and less deviance.

Third-box thinking, the boss, the employee and "the middle ground"

Let's go back to our earlier scenario, with the verbally oriented manager and her subordinate who prefers the written word. If the first box is the manager's preference for verbal exchange, and the second box is the employee's fondness for written communication, it's meaningful to note that the optimal scenario, in fact, resides in a third box.

Third Box Influencing Process

- Their world , "Them"
- Their drives
- Their behaviours
- Their energy level
- Their decision styles

- Our world , "We"
- Our drives in motion
- Our behaviours
- Our energy level
- Our decision styles

- Your world , "Me"
- My drives
- My behaviours
- My energy level
- My decision styles

Source: the Predictive Index®, a registered trademark of Predictive Index LLC and used here with permission.

At one of his presentations, the famous American motivator and trainer Zig Ziglar once shared with me that "a leader can get anything he wants in business if he helps enough other people get what they want." This stuck with me for over thirty years. He was bang on. Your best deals, your best projects, your best employees all came from what I call this third-box arrangement or thinking.

Third-box thinking is the very particular strategy that favors neither one nor the other world but, instead, imagines a third scenario wherein the identified idiosyncrasies and inclinations of each world are fully present and engaged, but in a neutral place where the two styles can find productive correlation. In third-box thinking, neither an individual's communication style nor his personal set of organically accumulated predispositions is diminished. They are, rather, exploited to optimal effect.

In other words, the manager keen to solve a particular business problem or advance his agenda in a certain direction does himself no favors if he blusters into the challenge with his ego fully cocked. After all, he's presumably invested time, energy and expense into onboarding and training the individual with whom he seeks to connect. How foolish would it be then to burn all that effort by insisting all communication takes place inside his box?

We've been dealing with a national food company whose CEO is very much what we call an "assertive ambivert." That means he is highly technical and values detail. A tuned-in person always shows up at a meeting with this guy with all the particulars on the table explored and accounted for. And he understands that whatever you have to say to this leader better be said in a way that respects the process. But this guy's successor lives according more to what we consider a "torpedo pattern." That means he is very persuasive, but also very impatient. The details-oriented CEO frustrated him, a person who could hit the moon or miss by 200,000 miles. When he's on, he's bang on, but when he's off, he's way off.

In the end, the new guy and the old guard could find no common ground (or third box), and parted ways. As clever and energetic as the new guy was, he simply was not attentive to the chairman's need to be very decisively presented to, nor to his requirement for a certain level of planning, structure and data. That the pair could not elevate their relationship to the third box was a shame, because they could've complemented each other effectively. Mindful leaders are responsible also for the good they do not do. Ignoring good data to do good coaching is reckless. Analytics allow leaders to get close or proximate with their people in a real and genuine way.

I have seen the use of science-based analytics software like the Predictive Index accelerate this third-box concept. Analytics plus what I like to call the boss/leader's "golden gut" or intuition leads to much better outcomes. You need the data to help you approach the other person's world. Also, the data cannot be a twenty- or thirty-page report or a special meeting with a PhD costing thousands of dollars.

The company vision

Third-box thinking could also be tied in to what an entire organization's values or vision is. Maybe these home in on integrity, respect or accountability. Maybe they celebrate entre-preneurial spirit or family values, or the loud and constant call for a disciplined approach to business. Whatever. The cultiva-tion of these defining corporate features is a critical part of the corporate DNA. From my experience, it is usually the most senior person — the chairman, the founder — who decides what the company's vision will be. It is, at last, a reflection of their own vision.

The Productivity Ambition Matrix

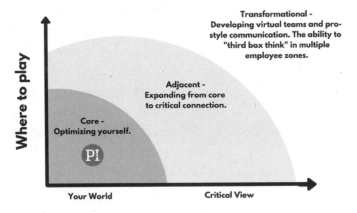

Source: the Predictive Index®, a registered trademark of Predictive.Index LLC and used here with permission.

From the illustration above, I like to think about the core of each person. To assist us to really understand an employee or colleague, I like to use the Predictive Index survey. This is a wonderful peek at the personality core of a person. Next, leaders are wise to think about what I call the productivity ambition matrix (ROI P). This series of adjacent half circles helps leaders think about their critical connection to their direct reports and their teams. When leaders think from the world of their critical connections, they start to develop what we call transforma-tional leadership. This I call "third-box thinking." It is made wonderfully easier when we add in predictive analytics like the very cool software from the Predictive Index.

Whatever it is, this "blueprint of the organization" is often grandly put on the wall, there to declare nothing less than the company's personality. But it is just as often never explained to the individuals whose comprehension of it is so important and, worse, never lived, never executed. Intended to offer the entire staff a view into where the operation is going, the corporate mission needs to find effective passage into every leader's psyche if it is ever to be embraced. Because if a leader isn't mindful of these stated corporate beliefs — because maybe they exist somewhere outside of his personal ego — he won't live his company's vision. He will prove himself incapable of transcending the box of his world into the box of the corporate values. And so no third-box approach will present itself that might have been able to see this important mission through.

That they sometimes can't is not a surprise. Achieving third-box thinking is not as simple as it seems. For a manager to transport himself to that impartial territory where very discrete sets of lifestyles, backdrops and cultivated personality types find common purchase, he must shed the ego he might imagine to be the central characteristic that delivered him to the managerial role. To engage with others, it is necessary for the leader to genuinely appreciate that his is not the right, best and only way to approach a situation. And achieving such a state of selflessness — the hallmark of a mindful manager — is not a walk in the park.

Yoga breaths

The ascent of mindfulness as a peace-bestowing approach to personal management has gone hand in hand with the ascent of yoga. This once highly marginalized instrument of well-being enhancement is now as mainstream as a turn at the gym or a retreat into nature. Given that, the concept of a "yoga breath" should be as accepted as reflexively understood.

Here is where a manager is practicing mindfulness at its most basic level. Rather than behaving in a reactionary manner to a situation that favors his natural inclination to hear only his own ego, a mindful manager is reflective of his actions and motivations. Often, this philosophy arises from his dedication to build a pause into every consideration of everything. To take a "yoga breath" is to hesitate before saying or doing something one might later realize was not reflective of his more mindful version of self.

By adopting such a built-in period of reflection, a manager might recognize that his impulse reaction is more about satisfying his ego than anything else, and that a truly mindful appreciation for the situation at hand would be more productive. Now the new-age mindful manager can get instant feedback on how their culture is being perceived, with the real-time data provided by Glassdoor, a company that allows employees, past and present, to rate both the leader and how the company treats its employees. Glassdoor found that, in the third quarter of 2016, 47 percent of employees felt confident that in the next six months they would find a new position suitable for their experience level.

One big arena to which this oversight applies is hiring. Too often, managers rely only on their gut to hire, and that's a bad thing. I had a client recently who worked for a government agency in Ottawa. They were looking for an executive vice president to handle their auditing operations, and had narrowed the pool down to a shortlist of two. One candidate was internal, and the other came from one of the big banks and so had a much more impressive pedigree on this front. But the hiring team was thorough in their selection. Rather than snap up the bank guy for his arguably more applicable and executive-level experience, they paused and asked themselves: "Who is going to be better suited for the requirements of the job? Who could we set up to be the best version of themselves in this post? Is it actually smarter to pick the bank guy, who is persuasive and makes lightning-fast decisions but maybe doesn't have any particularly thoughtful impulses in an audit position?" In the end, they were mindful and analytical in their response. They took a collective yoga breath, adopted some third-box thinking and hired the other guy.

A leader's authenticity

Mindfulness — according to Jon Kabat-Zinn, a world-renowned expert in the field — is about being in a relationship with yourself from both an inner and an outer viewpoint. It's about understanding your core patterns and being more aware of the space outside your own personalities. Dr. Kabat-Zinn writes, "Wherever you go, there you are." Leaders who are lost in thought and distraction are not fully present and so don't enjoy a chance to be fully aware. Mindfulness is often a hostage to our daily agendas. It really is about bringing things into greater focus.

Education, health care, the military and the sporting world entered the age of mindfulness before the business and leadership world did. But we're getting there now, with leaders genuinely appreciating that mindfulness must be a key piece of their leadership kitbag. It truly is a mindfulness revolution. Leaders today must begin to practice mindfulness.

And they must appreciate that workers are really looking for authenticity in their leaders. An authentic leader is self-aware and congruent. They don't see the need to change for anyone. They are aware that change could be tough for them, and that the journey to the top of the house is necessarily going to be a challenge. They are assertive, they can multitask, they don't get stuck in details and they can pivot. That last point is important. The job at the top of the house is dynamic, and so the person occupying it needs to be flexible on his feet.

Employees want to be understood by their superiors. They want to be guided by bosses who are able to get off the old-school leadership treadmill and lead others from a self-aware place. Leaders who can stop long enough to really be "there" in conversations with their employees will get higher engagement scores and, according to science, be healthier at work.

Still, the authentic leader has assertiveness and the desire to win with people, but also the wisdom to know when to start and when to stop. Most authentic leaders have a great deal of empathy. And that's empathy, mind, not sympathy. In the social profit world, sympathy is best used between family members, but empathy is best used between a leader and her co-workers.

All of this plays into authenticity. Wisdom traditions like mindfulness are now being aligned with science to show new potential that leaders at work can leverage. The eradication of impulsive leadership will remove enormous amounts of harm and conflict from the workplace.

Chapter 2

The Mindfulness of Communication

"We think that we have successful communication
with others. In fact, we only have successful miscom-
munication without being aware of it."

— DZONGSAR JAMYANG KHYENTSE RINPOCHE

Communication is something in which we all engage on a daily
basis — with the Starbucks barista, the transit worker, the neigh-
bors and co-workers we encounter en route to the office. But
believe at your peril that the time we spend communicating in
any way guarantees our mastery of it. More often than not, our
conversations are by rote and formality. Cruise-control responses
to cruise-control questions. How are you? Fine. How are you?
Fine. Done. Mindful communication fail. Unmindful communication — a practice that can cause all kinds of problems, including
costly misunderstandings, inefficient use of time, ugly alienation,
painful frustration and so on — continues its reign.

Living mindfully isn't all about practicing meditation and gratitude. It's also about participating in a conscious commitment to

have effective, compassionate, empathetic, productive engagements with other people. It's about connecting with meaning and intention, about being present, about listening well and speaking deliberately. It's about shedding ego and applying targeted attention and awareness with your words and actions. And it's about feeling positive and complete in all your communication with the folks in your world.

There's no shortage of research across a breadth of fields — psychology and neuroscience prominent among them — that demonstrates the value of meaningful connections in our lives. Humans are social animals to the core. We simply *like* to be with other people. We seek them out, we talk with them, we plan with them, we work with them. We are endlessly social with them. And, ideally, that social stuff is enveloped in a layer of sophistication. Our most important evolutionary edge, after all, is our ability to cooperate with others in complex social networks. We even have a hormone — oxytocin — that courses through our veins (particularly during breastfeeding, sex and caregiving) expressly to build and strengthen social bonds. This social imperative extends into the workplace, where individuals' well-being is generously assisted by a sense of harmony with those around them. Mastering effective communication is key to this ideal.

Effective communication is a requisite part of any healthy relationship, whether among romantic partners, family members, friends or co-workers. On a larger scale, this flesh-and-blood essential is fundamental to the peace and prosperity of our society as a whole. You only have to check your Twitter feed or watch a burst or two of news to bear witness to the damage that's done when something's misunderstood. There's no shortage of situations out there — personal, professional, political — that could have been rescued or sidestepped entirely if the people involved had put more thought and consideration into their communication skills.

In a mindfully lived existence, everyone is as active a listener as they are a contributor. They have an open mind, and no interest in manipulating a conversation or predicting its outcome. They're focused on the "we" needs, as opposed to the "me" needs. These are people with a mindful presence, meaning they've let go of results, a move that tends to eliminate emotional outbursts or overreacting. They're keen and compassionate and alive to the requirements and vibes of those around them.

What is mindful communication?

Mindful communication is the application of the tenets of mindfulness, as discussed earlier, to our relations with others. By communicating more mindfully with those we encounter in our personal and professional lives, we change the way we speak and listen, enhance our relationships and create connection and opportunities for engagement and meaning. We also achieve our goals (or at least increase our chances of same), thanks to our effective, explicit expressions thereof.

The art of communication is about more than sharpening your public-speaking and writing skills — a fact sometimes overlooked. Mindful communication has less to do with capturing your listeners' attention effectively and more to do with engaging with your communication partners effectively.

In her book, *The Five Keys to Mindful Communication*, Susan Chapman highlights silence, mirroring, encouraging, discerning and responding. Taken as a whole, the quintet works to foster deeper listening skills, along with the resources for responding with clarity and confidence.

In mindful communication, participants listen and speak with compassion, kindness and awareness. (This distinguishes it from the more conventional understanding of conversation, which *Merriam-Webster* suggests is "the imparting or interchange of thoughts, opinions, or information by speech, writing, or signs"

— a definition that features precisely no mention of compassion or kindness.) People in this more evolved scenario think before they speak, and share their thoughts with considered deliberation for how they will be received. They are truly present in the moment; they are curious, kind, nonjudgmental as they listen. And when they speak, they do it honestly and respectfully, and always mindful of whether what they share is useful to its recipients. Surely, you can see how this would be helpful in the workplace!

Randy at Microsoft was adept at this. He never listened to gossip, ever. He truly went to listening mode before judgment. In one case, our team had sold a large software subscription contract with a buyout clause that could be executed at the end. The contract ran for six years, and then the buyout. My team had done all their work well, and the client was happy. However, a buyout at Microsoft was seen as a "loss." Finance would not pay commissions on this event. It was a sale but deemed a loss. Randy listened to all sides and then, since he did not agree with the decision, set up a direct meeting between our team and the president of Microsoft Canada. This was an act of true skillfulness with all participants.

"Mindful communication" is a term that originated in Buddhist philosophy. It became popular in the West thanks to the efforts of Dr. Kabat-Zinn, who created the Stress Reduction Clinic and the Center for Mindfulness in Medicine, Health Care, and Society at the University of Massachusetts Medical School. A student of Buddhist teachers such as Thich Nhat Hanh and a founding member of the Cambridge Zen Center, the good doctor is credited with introducing the medical profession to the idea that meditation could help their patients reduce stress and other physical ailments. He encouraged the union of Eastern and Western concepts in treating stress, anxiety, pain and illness. Dr. Kabat-Zinn's efforts resulted in his creation of a mindfulness-based stress reduction program offered by medical centers, hospitals and health-maintenance organizations around the US.

Why mindful communication's important

Ask a lawyer. They'll tell you about the misunderstandings and absence of effective communication that haunt the core of so many lawsuits. People agree to do something. They sign papers with a flourish and shake hands with muscular pleasure. Then one day it turns out that each party heard something completely different. Uh-oh.

Mindful communication is a good thing. It brings about harmony in relationships and harmony within yourself. At work, mindful communication can help you to think on your feet, seek out information in a collaborative manner, resolve conflict such that all parties feel heard and encourage transparency about processes. Get all of these things right and you'll improve relationships, enhance productivity and feel generally more engaged with colleagues and superiors. And when we feel more connected to the folks with whom we share our professional space, we're more likely to feel joyful, tapped in and satisfied at work. Studies also report that we suffer less stress and endure fewer health problems too.

What impedes mindful communication?

According to a recent Gallup study, 87 percent of employees worldwide feel disengaged at work. Issues with communication are at the root of much of this disengagement. At one level, this disconnect is ironic. After all, modern technology has seen to it that, at least in theory, we're always connected and forever reachable. The irony, though, is that we're never actually *present*. That's because, while digital connection provides unprecedented flexibility in our communication events, it can also expose us to the distractions of email, social media and any number of other bursts of device-sprung technology that can work to destabilize and subtly erode our presence.

Truly, there's a great number of obstructions that throw themselves up in the way of genuinely mindful communication. Many of them are habits and patterns we've learned and employed since our earliest days. Exchanging them for something more enlightened is always a good idea.

Here are some of the more common impediments to getting the mindful-communication trick right:

- You hear what you expect to hear rather than what's actually being said.
- Lack of empathy.
- Poor attention skills.
- Inattention.
- A tendency to jump to conclusions.
- An insistence that you get to talk.
- Distractions (and giving in to them).
- A proclivity for reactivity.

Reactivity versus proactivity

It's always better to be more proactive than reactive in one's communication techniques. Reactivity is simply lazy communication. Likes and smiles. Playing victim to the triggers of social media. Quick-hit, low-investment responses. Proactivity, on the other hand, calls for thoughtfulness and planning.

And then there's reflective communication, the next natural step along the continuum of engagement, and its requirement that you step back before talking to someone to collect your thoughts and determine your next move. In our world of predictive analytics, we can now run software like the Predictive Index to get data on who will be proactive as a leader and who will be a more harmonious boss. It is very difficult to make someone proactive in the long term if their drives and behaviors are reactive. It doesn't work.

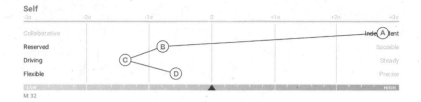

Example of a proactive leader
Source: the Predictive Index®, a registered trademark of Predictive Index LLC and used here with permission.

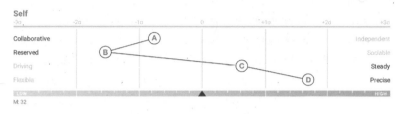

Example of a reactive leader
Source: the Predictive Index®, a registered trademark of Predictive Index LLC and used here with permission.

Steve Jobs is often held up as an exemplar of reflective communication in action. He's celebrated for the preparation time he would put into crafting his presentations. He would spend hours rehearsing his words and would take the time to infuse all that he said with very purposeful messaging.

Down in the trenches, we should always seek to create a mindful balance between reactive and reflective communication. Ideally, we are immediately responsive when the scene calls for it, and we are slow and thoughtful when it does too.

Let me hear your body talk

The importance of body language has long been noted in an endless parade of parsed-out appreciation for the component parts of communication. Body language carries 55 percent of our intent when we're conversing with others — a huge amount! Tone of voice accounts for 38 percent. The much-ballyhooed spoken word, meanwhile, only accounts for a lousy 7 percent!

First off, consider posture. The way a person holds himself has a lot to say about how he feels about himself and the person he's with. Is he leaning in toward the other person, or back and away? Mirroring someone's posture is a good way to create rapport. It will happen naturally in some situations. Try it out — but don't make it too obvious or it can be off-putting. What is the posture of someone who feels confident? We have all seen social psychologist Amy Cuddy's wonderful TED Talk on this. How does someone sit/stand when they feel threatened or fearful? Body language affects how others see us, but it may also change how we see ourselves. Cuddy argues in favor of "power posing" — standing in a posture of confidence, even when we don't feel confident. I have seen introvert boss/leaders who practice body language boost their feelings of confidence and dramatically impact their presentations.

If you feel nervous about a presentation you have to give, adopt a posture of confidence and think yourself into a positive mode. See what a difference it makes. Your personality (your Predictive Index is always you) and your body language can and should be "altered" for the situation.

Hand gestures are another interesting aspect of body language that can show attitudes and emotions. An open palm signifies sincerity, openness. Steepling the fingers is seen as authoritative, or used during negotiation when considering a proposal. Tapping or drumming the fingers shows impatience. Touching your face indicates thinking. Touching your hair broadcasts insecurity. Touching your ears signals indecision.

It's worth pointing out that electronic communication, which excludes the all-important physical element, deprives our modern world of a great deal of critical communicative nuance. But we already knew that.

Communication and workplace analytics

Workplace analytics and tools like the Predictive Index produce personality data that help companies to identify the most effective means of communicating with one another. People who rate a high B on the Predictive Index are very visual, for example, so that requirement needs to be taken into consideration when communicating with these individuals. One of my daughters, the one who works at Deloitte, is an ambivert. Sometimes she'll be persuasive and sometimes she'll be technical — that's just who she is. Meanwhile, my other daughter is very altruistic. She has to see what impact a decision she might make will have on other people.

Every personality has a different path to communication. That's where analytics come in. It determines a style of communication in which we're most comfortable. And it's very interesting to watch. There are hallway-chat people, book-it-in-Outlook people (don't ask them to weigh in on football scores) and everyone in between. Some folks have a preference for email. Others love getting handwritten letters. Some people will only talk to you on the phone.

We had a project with Hill's pet food recently that had much to reveal about this kind of thing. They closed a lot of their offices and introduced a freelance environment for their salespeople. But they had a lot of high-B persuasive salespeople on staff, and it turned out that this style of operating wasn't the most effective for them. I had one guy call me to say he had started hanging around coffee shops because he had to be around people — a fact that had not been considered when they closed their offices. The communication that had been so natural in the office environment stopped. A lot of sales teams now will bring in Skype because they simply have to be seen to communicate.

I work with two very different McDonald's operators. Todd and Marcia Finlayson have become world-class operators who have amassed numerous awards for customer experience and growth. Their communication style is proactive; they are "builders." They create cultural champion leaders in their dynamic organization, the Finlayson Hospitality Partners. They lead extremely well and, guess what? Their employees love working for them. Their restaurants are among the top McDonald's operations in North America, and both Todd and Marcia were recently recognized for raising money for Ronald McDonald House. Both have a high level of persuasiveness and collaboration and are alike on lots of other fronts besides — how they communicate most notable among them.

At the Ronald McDonald House event, it was interesting to anticipate which one of them would be the first to reach for the trophy. When these two are aligned, they're fabulously aligned. But when they fight, it's like two bulls, and everybody knows they're going to see stars. Their communication is so alike that the egos are almost the same. That's hard to manage sometimes. When personalities are the same, there's a tremendous upside,

Marcia and Todd Finlayson, award-winning owner-operators of McDonald's Restaurants (Finlayson Hospitality Partners, Toronto).
Source: Photo courtesy of Ronald McDonald House Canada.

but there's also a tremendous battle-zone potential for conflict. They have both the same needs and drives.

This communication distinction may be tied in to how we're all seen in our tribes. We all have our own tribes, and communication styles associated with them. There are visual tribes (who want Excel spreadsheets), technical tribes (who want computer-generated stats), builder tribes (interested in how to win, make change happen and boast about it afterward) and, in the middle of it all, altruistic tribes. The fact is that your message might only be received if it's delivered in a certain way. The mindful manager is good at matching communication style with worker, and at adjusting all day long.

The art of listening well

Epictetus wasn't fooling around when he said, "We have two ears and one mouth so that we can listen twice as much as we speak." More recently, businessman and author Stephen Covey enhanced the concept with an admonition that we "seek to understand first, then to be understood." That means laboring to sympathize with the other person's perspective. It means tamping down irritation and generally being more concerned with being happy than being right.

Poor listening is behind a thousand of our headaches and heartaches. From failed relationships and poor grades to lost customers and misrouted deliveries, listening could not play a more critical role in our day-to-day existence.

Enter mindful listening, and its power to set straight both sides of a communication exchange. Here, brain power is a key ingredient, kicking in to improve concentration, memory and focus. When you listen mindfully, the quality of your listening supports the other person to be more present, at ease, collaborative and genuine. Conversations conducted in this manner can be more meaningful and productive than the mindless alternative.

Deep and mindful listening encourages others to feel heard and to speak more openly and honestly in return. Among the biggest problems with communication is that we often fall into the trap of listening not to understand but to reply. In the former, we hear without interrupting, asking questions, agreeing or otherwise injecting any speech. If you can truly hear another person's message — different from simply sitting silent till you can next open your trap — you'll have taken the first step toward mindful communication.

Good listening also means allowing yourself the time and space to fully absorb what people are saying. It's looking not just at the surface meaning of someone's words but at where they're genuinely coming from — what personal need or interest is motivating their speech. Listening requires a combination of intention and attention. In *Mindful Magazine,* author David Rome sums up this concept thus: "The intention part is having a genuine interest in the other person — their experiences, views, feelings, and needs. The attention part is being able to stay present, open, and unbiased as we receive the other's words — even when they don't line up with our own ideas or desires."

Some other tips for effective listening:

- **Clear your intent** so you have nothing else to do but be with that person in that moment. When someone starts to talk to you, do your best to empty your brain of its ghosts. Put away assumptions, preconceptions and expectations. Be whole and total and engaged.
- **Put aside physical distractions** like your cellphone, tablet and computer.
- **Shut off notifications** on your devices.
- Pay attention to the speaker's **tone and body language**. What are they *really* saying?

- **Be vigilant** with your focus. If your mind wanders to other topics, coax it back to the person across from you.
- **Don't assume.** If the person who's talking says something you don't understand or isn't very clear, don't jump to any conclusions (and get all reactive). Ask him to clarify his statement. There's nothing wrong with posing questions as long as you ask them with compassion. Let go of your own agenda and home in on the other person's needs and wants.
- Take a **mindful breath** before responding.
- **Broaden your awareness** so you're open to the full range of information coming your way, including tone of voice and body language.
- **Resist the urge to interrupt** — let the other person share their full thoughts before jumping in with your own.
- **Be curious.** Ask open-ended questions that encourage dialogue.

Speaking mindfully

Having mastered the listening side of things, here's how you look after the mindful-speaking stuff. **Mindful speaking** is about speaking from a place of truth, and not from a place where the goal is only to *win*. When you're speaking mindfully, you're not exaggerating, lying or projecting nervous energy onto the other person. You're being true and authentic. And you're working from the heart.

The yoga pause is important here. Practice taking a beat before you speak. When someone asks you a question, don't just start talking. Take a lungful of breath and consider what you're about to let loose from your voice box. Notice what it feels like to not say something that risks any kind of damage. Your taking time to ponder a question is a great gift to the person who asked it.

Some other advice for mindful speaking:

- **Choose your words consciously.** Just because something makes sense to you doesn't automatically confer sense on it for others. Hear the words in your head first, and imagine possible scenarios that might backfire from their uttering.
- **Be sincere.** Assume that everything you say to someone else is being taken at face value. If you pledge to do something, really mean to do it. As the Buddhists say, "Word, thought and deed have to be one." Whether in business or personal life, keeping your word goes a long way.
- **Clarify your intentions.** You need to be clear on what you want to get out of an interaction before you enter into it. Reflect on that first, then. The surer your intentions, the easier it will be to get to the point.
- **Be succinct.** The muddier you make your language, the less directly accessible is your argument.
- **Speak from yourself.** It's important to make your conversational case from a position of ownership — i.e., with the "I" language rather than accusatory "you make me feel," which can get the listener's back up.
- **Make yourself useful.** If it's always clear that your engagement in a discussion is to be helpful and contribute mindfully, that can only further the scene.
- **Practice non-judgment.** If you're able to stay open and suspend judgment in a social engagement, you will be in a position to respond wisely and more artfully. When we start to make assumptions about our communication with a particular person, or bring our preconceived ideas about their meaning or motivations, we get into trouble. As a CEO, it's easy to get stuck in a judging role because people look to you to make judgments every day. The

problem is that judgmental communication is not best for learning. To mindfully converse and avoid conflicts, we need to try our best to refrain from evaluating and drawing conclusions on the other person's opinion, story or perspective. We should come to terms with the fact that there are always two sides to the story, and that neither one of them is necessarily right or wrong.

- **Demonstrate understanding.** All anybody wants, as Oprah Winfrey has so famously said, is to be *known*. The importance of showing others that we understand them cannot be undervalued. That means having statements like "I understand" and "I see what you mean" at the ready. The comfort of such reassurances cannot be undervalued.
- **Be empathetic.** Climbing into someone else's shoes is the best thing for ensuring an environment of compassionate understanding. To show this kind of empathy is to respect their experience. Experiences are relative, after all. People react and see things based only and always on how they view the world.
- **Be present.** The gift of your undivided presence is the best you can offer in a mindful conversation. That means not checking your phone or mentally drifting. Focus is an art. Master it meaningfully.
- **Be generous.** If the first things out of your mouth after your conversational partner has spoken are about you, you failed the mindfulness test. Sharing a personal story, however charming or exciting, is not the correct response to someone else's exposition. It reveals that you were likely just sitting on your own stuff until the other guy ran out of wind, and that you don't really care much to hear it at all.
- **Maintain eye contact.** Don't look at your feet or your phone when someone's talking to you. Look only into your conversational partner's eyes. It shows that you care — wouldn't you want someone to do the same for you?

- **Be conscious of habits.** How we respond to others is largely a function of habit. We all develop small automatic responses over the course of our lives that shape the way we communicate with others. Being aware of patterns of thinking that lead to arguments and anger is the first step. Without awareness, these patterns go unnoticed and impact on our communication. So be aware of the role your past experiences and conditions play in your communications. Break patterns that lead to arguments, anger or less-than-ideal communication.

Mindful communication requires practice, but the results are worth every bit of exertion. The only way to have people respect you is if you respect them, and engaging in effective communication using mindfulness is one of the best methods for earning that respect.

Ray Dalio, one of the world's most successful investors and entrepreneurs, has written a seminal success-in-life manual, *Principles,* which has been downloaded multiple millions of times for its undeniable wisdom in applying sound principles to everything, including a pursuit of a meaningful work life. Some highlights:

- Recognize that effective, innovative thinkers are going to make mistakes.
- Get over "blame" and "credit" and get on with "accurate" and "inaccurate."
- When you experience pain, remember to reflect.
- Be assertive and open-minded at the same time.
- Ask yourself whether you have earned the right to share an opinion.
- Distinguish open-minded people from closed-minded people.

Chapter 3

Being Mindful in Retention

"You cannot manage other people unless you manage yourself first."

— PETER F. DRUCKER

Today's employees want to be understood, and treated accordingly. That means they need to be led by bosses who are able to get off the old-school leadership treadmill and lead others by way of a process that is sublimely self-aware. Leaders who can stop long enough to really be present in their interactions with their employees will get higher engagement scores and, says science, have more robust experiences in their work life. Oh, and best of all? They'll keep the workers they've got on the payroll because they'll be happy as hens to be there.

Hiring a staff is one thing. There's an electricity to the achievement of employment, after all, and that holds true for both sides of the big mahogany desk. The air fairly thrums with the victory of it all, the delicious busy-ness of onboarding, the energy of launching a new adventure. But that celestial scene comes down to earth in pretty short order. In no time, the effervescent new employee has lost his lustre and joined the ranks of the merely employed. In some cases, it could be at this point that the thrill of the chase looms up again for this individual. And when it does, managers beware: this is an extremely threatening spectre for the company and its wished-for continuity. From my experience, most candidates are at their best behavior in the interview. The key is, who will they be ninety days after being hired?

That is why it is preferable, always, to continue to polish the sheen of this newcomer. Retention is the stable, emotionally evolved sibling to excitable, impulsive acquisition.

The concept of mindfulness has lots to offer in the area of retention. A manager who is psychically connected to his employees stands a much better chance of keeping them engaged than a manager who regards them as simply a means to his end. With mindfulness, we as leaders acknowledge our "bad boss" or negatron styles. By confronting them thus, we understand the harm we can visit on fellow employees at work. Mindfulness is the trick that lifts a staffer from utilitarian status to one that features a more comprehensive appreciation for their integration in a team effort.

A leader's authenticity

I met a municipal leader recently at a McDonald's restaurant. We were there to mark McHappy Day, an event that celebrates the company's charitable attention to sick kids and their families. The mayor of Markham, Ontario, a bustling suburb of Toronto, was having a Big Mac, shooting the breeze and genuinely enjoying himself. Frank Scarpitti is a wonderful leader. This is a guy you just know to be authentic because he has no airs about him. He took his jacket off and sat down in the midst of a buzzing group of people and was able to accept that all of us were different. Better still, he was able to calibrate his versions of self to best accommodate each of us.

He was talking to me, the owner of a software organization, and also to the owner-operator of nine McDonald's franchises. And then he had all these regular-folk constituents approaching him, as well, and he was able to connect with them too. I think current Toronto mayor, John Tory, struggles with this because of his blue-blood background. He's so stiff. He vacillates between being authentic and corporate. I think his predecessor, Rob Ford, like him or not, had a lot of the authentic-leader stuff in him. In his case, his focus was too large, his energy level was too large, his capacity to respond was too large, he had trouble focusing. There might be a case to be made for Donald Trump on this front, too, but I haven't the stomach to make it.

People leave a leader, not a company

When a leader starts a company, they're the number-one salesperson. That's the purest leadership model there is. Then other people start crowding the scene. Newcomers — the so-called "secondary salespeople" — arrive at the company, and while they may buy into the vision and feel compelled to follow this leader, each new layer means the message gets a little more lost. Unless the model is created so it's predictable and everyone who joins it has the same DNA as the founder, there will be challenges. So how can analytics create leader-followers whose DNA is close to the founder's?

See Chudleigh's, a very successful food manufacturer in Milton, Ontario, whose turnover is a measly 2 percent. That's because, at a very early stage in the company's development, they realized they needed analytics data to understand the model of who to hire and what a leader looks like. Software like the Predictive Index creates "people insurance" on who to add to the payroll and who to promote. Fast-growing Chudleigh's followed this proven approach for more than ten years, hiring, training and pushing buttons according to it. Here is a company that understands that the bottleneck is the leadership group.

Behavioral Drives

The PI Behavioral Assessment predicts four primary personality constructs (see below) and two secondary constructs (Factors E — Decision Making, and M — Response Level). These are "normal" (non-clinical) characteristics that describe, explain and predict day-to-day workplace behaviors.

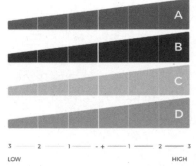

Dominance
HIGH: Independent, assertive and self-confident
LOW: Agreeable, cooperative and accommodating

Extraversion
HIGH: Outgoing, persuasive and socially-poised
LOW: Serious, introspective and task-oriented

Patience
HIGH: Patient, consistent and deliberate
LOW: Fast-paced, urgent and intense

Formality
HIGH: Organized, precise and self-disciplined
LOW: Informal, casual and uninhibited

3 —— 2 —— 1 —— - + —— 1 —— 2 —— 3
LOW   HIGH

Source: the Predictive Index®, a registered trademark of Predictive Index LLC and used here with permission.

The number-one reason people leave companies is not money — money's number four or five on the list. Number one is: do I have a friend at work? After that, they're interested in being rewarded based on their DNA, a fact that escapes most leaders, who default to recognizing and rewarding all employees the same way. That's a problem. If you're a team player who doesn't want to be singled out onstage, you're going to disengage if you're not understood and treated appropriately. You're going to have more accidents, not show up at work, get into deviant activity and so on.

Retention is about physically being there, being alert and active, and not leaving to go somewhere else. There are so many opportunities for young people out there right now. Unemployment is at 5 percent. Labor availability is flatlining in North America, and jobs are increasing. Meanwhile, in 2022,

25 percent of the North American workforce will be more than fifty-five years old. In 2018 in Canada, there was a 10.8 percent increase in demand for managers, a 21.3 percent increase in demand for roles that require university education, and a 34.4 percent increase in demand for roles that require college education/trades. This is creating a tremendous demand on people.

That's where analytics, with the power it lends to be more unique in a selection process, kicks in. Clever managers know they have to look for the skinny resume (people who might not have all the skills but might have the right drives and behaviors), and be more creative in talent acquisition than ever.

Empathy trumps sympathy

Most authentic leaders possess a great deal of empathy, a characteristic that needs to be distinguished from sympathy. Sympathy, you see, sucks margins out of businesses. If you're a sympathetic leader, you're forever at risk of going native. In other words, there is always the chance that you'll turn into one of *them*, whatever "them" might be. Empathy, on the other hand, is understanding. It's recognizing emotions in others, and working to climb inside their perspective and reality. Essentially, it's a return to the your-world/my-world third-box thinking.

In business, empathy is always preferable to sympathy. Sympathy keeps the borders up; empathy trashes them. Sympathy inspires one-dimensional thinking; empathy is multidimensional. Where a sympathetic leader might say, "Let's just give them what they need because it's the right thing to do," an empathetic leader might say, "They have a different way of thinking; maybe we should consider it."

Any conversation about retaining employees needs to consider the value of the empathetic approach. All of us wandering this planet, after all, share a singular requirement: to be acknowledged. To be recognized. To be *known*. The empathetic leader gets this and makes an effort to honor his subordinates with an ongoing recognition of this reality. He is real with them, and they, in turn, are real back. Cool new predictive software can help you identify potential leaders who have empathy — again, the Predictive Index is our choice of software here.

Mindfulness, all around.

According to Predictive Success, the best factors for predicting a leader are as follows:

- 1 percent education;
- 7 percent reference checks;
- 10 percent emotional intelligence;
- 12 percent GPA;
- 21 percent integrity tests;
- 34 percent interviews;
- 58 percent behavioral and cognitive interviews.

The day-by-day diligence of mindfulness

Wisdom traditions like mindfulness are now being aligned with science to reveal new potential for leaders in the workplace to leverage. The first question these individuals need to ask themselves is how they will approach and experience each day. One more Tuesday is just one more Tuesday, to be sure, but when history remembers each of us a thousand Tuesdays from now, it will be the essence of our efforts that will rise to the surface. When a great team is remembered for its special qualities years after it disperses, the personality at the helm is often the reason. Such individuals are remembered as fair, objective and human. Their teams will stick with them through thick Tuesdays and thin.

When I was with Microsoft, we built a fantastic new business team in the financial services unit that quickly racked up numerous victories to its name. This was over fifteen years ago, but each and every member of that team is still, to this day, in touch with the original leader of the group, Frank Vella. Frank created a legacy of leaders after him. His teams always performed well and he left his successor, Randy Lenaghan, a fantastic team. Frank, who spent ten years with Microsoft as managing director/general manager of the financial services group, was an extremely self-aware leader who practiced the art of mindfulness with his team abundantly. He worked on sales, services and industry solutions with a particular focus on capital markets, banking and insurance clients. He successfully established a significant market presence for the company in the financial services industry, displacing some long-standing competitors and meeting some aggressive growth benchmarks along the way. And he is remembered today for growing a world-class business unit that achieved high levels of operational performance.

Cut down all the business-speak about this accomplished guy and you'll find a home truth: Frank Vella achieved all of his success because he infused his interactions with his people with a great deal of mindfulness. This is a guy who treated everyone around him with respect, who heard others' points of view meaningfully and who adjusted his presence to accommodate other people constantly. His professional successes were a direct result of his personal ones.

Frank offers us a compelling example of mindfulness in action. It is through his example that we understand the enduring power of a mindful leader's ability to keep his subordinates and team members in close, steadfast touch. Because this was a man who always made a point of making contact with others and demonstrating a genuine caring for their lot, his people paid him back with devotion and constancy. A lesser leader who failed to engage with his crew in an authentic way would almost certainly be long forgotten by them fifteen years after the fact.

The dangers of impulsive leadership

Leaders like Frank Vella understand that successful companies, and the groups operating within them, require a strong manager leading the charge. That means an individual with, among a host of other critical characteristics, powerful planning and organizational skills. But what of the leaders who exhibit decidedly impulsive tendencies? What does this way of being bring to bear on these managers' ability to retain staff members?

Impulsive leaders are the folks who spring into action on a dime, and whose decisions are more likely to be made in a flash than contemplated for any length of time. While impulsive behavior has its undeniable positives (think about it: how much more fun is the guy who jumps at a chance for opportunistic engagement than the guy who's endlessly weighing his alternatives?), companies pay a price for having spontaneous, reckless managers in their midst. One of the most significant disadvantages of impulsive management behavior is that it can lead to destabilization in the workplace. Impulsive managers rewrite their expectations constantly and offer employees no real level of consistency regarding what is expected of them. With no reliable understanding of the reception their actions will inspire, these managers leave staffers to guess how and when they should act in certain situations.

More than making the manager-employee relationship feel decidedly tenuous, such an absence of understood expectations can leave employees fearful of their own place within the company. An impulsive manager could fire an employee on a whim. That kind of instability engenders performance that derives from a place of necessity and survival only — not a productive impulse to improve and expand. And employees in these situations do not do their jobs out of loyalty to their manager, but out of fear of losing their livelihoods or suffering some other unknown punitive consequences.

Not good.

Managers who act impulsively also tend to lack focus. They move from one task to the next and back again, reacting erratically to superficial cues and failing to bear down on any progressive project. These types of managers have no real sense of organization and do not prioritize their activities. And, critically, this lack of focus can prove corporately contagious. A leader who does not lead with a sense of purpose can very quickly find himself sitting atop an organization populated by similarly disinclined souls. Employees who have not been set on a path with a delegated and designated collection of expectations will not know which tasks should get priority treatment. The result could be certain chaos. Whatever goals a staff operating in this environment achieves probably achieve them by accident.

More than that, the spiritual and psychological status of workers toiling under the leadership of an impulsive manager needs to be taken into consideration. It is a blessing to feel confident in one's assignments, direction and expectations. It is a tyranny to come into work every day and not have a solid grasp on what you're responsible for completing. Such inexact management can damage a person's sense of self-esteem and ability to actualize into an accomplished whole. For a company concerned about holding on to its staffers, the importance of considering the effects of an impulsive, imprecise manager cannot be understated.

Managers who practice the art and science of rational, deliberated business management tend to be more successful in the long run. They get more done, and so do their employees. Better still, the people who work for them feel directed, acknowledged and nourished and so are inclined to stay with the company.

The manager as coach

Just like the body after a period of stress or effort, the mind needs rest. I was involved in a car accident a year ago that really rattled me. My Mercedes was totalled, and I was diagnosed as having a concussion. The advice I got from the doctors I saw post-crash was to go in a dark, quiet room, because my mind needed a chance to catch up. There's now a great deal of evidence that says concussions require swift, ongoing and assiduous attention. In the old days, it was a shrug and a buddy-pat and you were back in the game. But when today's hockey players are knocked into the boards, they have to come off the ice and be analyzed. Oftentimes, they need to get away from the scene and reflect.

Alas, the same learning hasn't been fully adopted in the workplace. There, too, it's typically still: So, you had a tough run-in with your colleague? Oh, well, just get back in the game. But the participants in these interactions have suffered a concussion, every bit as much as the hockey players and I have. Why? Because it was an impact, a collision of communication styles. And that collision led to a jolt of bad reception from which you're not going to get any better without some kind of treatment. One can only surface from such on-the-job brain clashes with a yoga pause, a retreat into solitude and a subsequent reappearance with fresh insight. And, ideally, that revised insight will prominently feature an acknowledgment of one's prior failure to be mindful of the other person's world and motivations.

There's lots to be learned from sports analogies for leaders keen to embrace mindfulness in their professional lives. Coaches who tap into the profusion of powerful data points offered up through behavioral assessments can get more from their players than coaches who simply pick the best athletes and throw them into the game. Mindful coaches understand that certain individuals excel in certain situations, and that particular combinations of player types will elicit the best performances. Off the ice (or the track or the field or the court), the same value should be assigned to critical insights of team members' ambition, risk tolerance, relationship development and interaction style.

Chapter 4

Being Mindful in Letting Employees Go

"Hiring people is an art, not a science, and resumes can't tell you whether someone will fit into a company's culture."

— HOWARD SCHULTZ,
FORMER CHAIRMAN AND CEO, STARBUCKS

Terminating an employee is one of the most disagreeable and stress-riddled tasks in a manager's work bag. There are legal issues and the imperative to perform the unpleasantness according to the highest letter of the law. There are issues of optics, and how a boss's conduct in this arena will look to the rest of his workforce. Essential, too, is the taste the ex-employee will have in his mouth after the fact. There's no telling into whose orbit this person will next travel, and it's important that he bring with him a positive hit of what the organization is about, even if he's been let go from it. And none of this even touches on the whole issue of the damage a leader risks inflicting on another person's psyche — and his own — with this rejection. No wonder so many senior-level execs race to delegate this job to underlings.

But there is a strategy for tackling this ugly bit of business compassionately, legally, humanely and — yes — mindfully.

The writing on the wall

Employees are normally terminated for one of only a handful of reasons. The organization is downsizing, or the individual worker has gone against company policy, broken company rules or performed her job poorly. Of course, there are other, more nefarious actions that can get an employee canned. Maybe the guy is duping the company out of a paycheck by warming a seat without making any effort. An employee I like to call a "chair spinner" is out the door at 5:01 p.m., faster than you can say Andre De Grasse. Or maybe he's stealing from the company. At my golf course in the Toronto area, a bookkeeper stole over $125,000 from the corporate coffers. The challenge here was that the general manager was not on his game and didn't find out about the crime until well after it had taken place. When he did, he terminated the individual poorly, and now there's a lawsuit. Analytics, it should be noted, can prevent these bad hires. The manager who looks away or who doesn't use the data is only depriving his company of a better scenario.

One idea that a company in Arizona tried was, instead of firing, ignoring. Here, you're working with individuals who are not meeting their sales targets or are creating collateral with other employees — essentially, bulls in china shops. Or maybe it's a superstar who imagines herself to be above the rules. Either way, you've got to bring that worker back into the camp. So you stop supporting her, cut back on your one-on-one time with her, take away her resources and generally make the decision that this person will have to support herself. With this plan, you're looking for a glimmer of independence or assertion in the last ten miles of the race. It aligns with the millennial concept that says kids who have been pampered through their lives will seek that attention again through performance if you cut the pampering off.

Performance improvement is still very much in the plan with this method, which I call the "shock-and-awe" approach. And it has been shown to work. It brings the fear of God into some of these employees. It's protective, in terms of meeting legal obligations, and it's also prescriptive. It's like when you go to a doctor and say, "Hey, I don't feel good, here's what the issues are." And the doctor says, "Here's the recovery process. It's going to be thirty days of monitoring and a sixty-day check-in. If there's no change, it's going to be path to termination."

When we look at nirvana for the boss, all her employees are cultural champions, they just fit and are engaged and performing. However, we will always have employees who are not quite there yet. What do we do with those who are needing to be fixed? Heck, you hired them, they deserve a wee bit of a recovery plan. This is only fair. We can look to address the "silent killers," those employees who actually like working for you, yet are just not performing.

When I led a team at Microsoft, we were transitioning the business from just cool technology to an actual client ecosystem in which clients would trust us and do what we called enterprise contracts with strategic partnerships. This was a tough transition. We paid our staff very well, and they all wanted to stay with us to continue to collect on their stock options and grants, which became valuable over three to five years from a grant date. This created a group of silent killers.

Many of this old guard were strong technically or just lucky enough to have been hired when Microsoft was a start-up. As the company changed, so did our needs for new skill sets and new drives and behaviors. What we needed changed, and unfortunately, lots of the old guard just couldn't rise to the new journey. This created our challenge. What do we do? The employees loved the place, but they were not performing any longer. We had hired them, so we needed to deal with them. Performance was dragging, so our better boss/leaders dug in and presented performance improvement plans with real, measurable dates and activities to be monitored. We became serious, and it worked. Many employees saw that the country club was over and they had to return to accountability. Others were promoted to "customer" (that is, fired), and moved on to other companies or retired completely.

In any event, it's important to face the firing imperative head on. To delay in terminating a poorly performing worker is to make an expensive choice. That the organization will endure some unrest and disruption with his dismissal is a given, but those negatives rarely outweigh the cost of keeping the worker on the payroll. Prolonging a mis-hire is most importantly not fair to the individual.

The perfect termination

It is, on the face of it, tricky to imagine a "perfect termination." The subject is inherently unpleasant, after all. And it's made even more so if you're having to let someone go whom you've known and worked with for years. But if you embrace the undeniable distastefulness of the assignment and work to imagine the most ideal version of a letting-go, you can uncover a reasonable road map.

Let's consider what that might look like.

When you terminate a worker's employment, no matter the gentle language in which you couch the dismissal, you're telling him that he's failed. That's going to hurt. More than a source of income, a job typically provides us with a sense of identity and self-esteem, to say nothing of the access it provides us to social networks. Understand that, and understand that a career transition of any sort is one of the most unsettling experiences you can face in your life.

Still, there are compassionate tactics a manager can employ to offer the person a gentle landing. Aim for one of those touchdowns at O'Hare Airport that draws a spontaneous eruption of applause from the passengers in the cabin. Such an approach can mitigate the trauma for the employee in a way that satisfyingly aligns with your organization's values. More than that, a thoughtfully planned termination not only works to ensure that employees leave your organization on the most positive terms possible but safeguards your reputation as a desirable employer and minimizes the incident's impact on the rest of your employees.

Authenticity plays a serious role in one's ability to pull this off. A manager who undertakes the task in a way that honors the gravity of the occasion will fare much better than someone who undermines its significance. After all, a person's job is at stake. It's important that the individual wielding the knife acknowledge that with their actions and words. The key message should be "this job is not a fit for you," so that the person's dignity can remain intact.

Sometimes people will be too clinical in their terminations, preferring to follow a performance-review mentality. God knows why, given the increasingly bad rap performance reviews suffer. A new Adobe survey that measured 1,500 American employees' and employers' responses to the things found that 22 percent of staffers have cried at least once afterward, and 20 percent found the experience so tough they had to quit. Sixty-plus percent of managers, meanwhile, call the review process outdated and claim the time they spend prepping for one negatively impacts their ability to do their jobs.

And yet the performance-review termination is a no-brainer, which is why some take that route. It's way easier, after all, to steer clear of the soft stuff with a focus on the hard. But as much as it might be a relief to the manager to home in on cold details, thereby distancing himself from the implicit discomfort of the assignment, it's eminently better to wade into the muck with the disenfranchised employee and spend some time with him there. And if it feels disagreeable — and it will — remind yourself that it's a hundred times more so for the person on the other side.

Tied up in this imperative is the requirement that the manager see through this uncomfortable task himself. In most situations, experts agree, the direct supervisor should be the one to deliver the bad news. By delegating a subordinate or a representative from the HR department to do the dirty work, you send a message that it doesn't rank as important to you. Or that you're too cowardly to face it yourself. Either way, it doesn't demonstrate regard for the soon-to-be-ex-employee getting the axe.

But as much as it's significant that the supervisor take the lead in this act of excision, the best practice is to have a third person in the room when that conversation takes place, ideally someone from HR. This way, the manager has a secondary source of information (to field questions on the layoff package, benefits, final paychecks, etc.), as well as a witness and an on-hand neutral buffer. Additionally, it's advisable to have a career-transition consultant on site to meet with departing employees following the announcement. This person can provide impartial, confidential support you may be ill equipped to offer, given the circumstances.

So the manager's got to be the person wearing the firing shoes. And there's no denying that she's going to feel uncomfortable to her soles. The only real trick to overcoming this reality is experience. The more dismissals in which a person participates, the better prepared she is to stare down another one. And if you don't have real-life experience, you can always invent it. To wit, you might practice firing a person, with a friend sitting in the hot seat, to rehearse not only your key messages but your demeanor. It's important that the person in the superior role exudes confidence around it. If there's any whiff of doubt in the room, the employee could interpret it as the company having made a mistake, a signal the employer doesn't want on the table. Mind you, if the manager is coping with nerves, it's not a disaster. It conveys to the employee that the decision was not an easy one to make.

We have found that when leaders use workforce analytics — software like the Predictive Index — it gives them a roadmap for the right way to approach a termination. For example, an employee with a high level of extraversion (Predictive Index high B) will need his ego protected and will be ready to try to persuade you that you are wrong. The employee who is very detailed and sequential (high D for detail and high C for patience) will need all the facts and a longer time to understand the situation, and the change will be much harder on them.

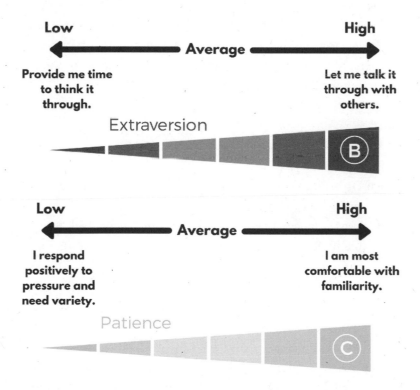

Low   **High**
Average

Provide me time   Let me talk it
to think it   through with
through.   others.

Extraversion

(B)

Low   **High**
Average

I respond   I am most
positively to   comfortable with
pressure and   familiarity.
need variety.

Patience

(C)

Source: the Predictive Index®, a registered trademark of Predictive Index LLC and used here with permission.

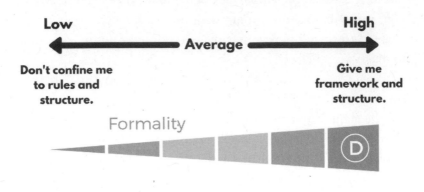

Low   **High**

◄———————— **Average** ————————►

**Don't confine me
to rules and
structure.**

**Give me
framework and
structure.**

Formality

D

Source: the Predictive Index®, a registered trademark of Predictive Index LLC and used here with permission.

Also, have your proxy rehearse the range of possible responses with which the individual might react to the news, in order that you're appropriately armed. Imagine what kind of questions the person might ask, and be ready with responses that are as compassionate as they are comprehensive.

Here is our list:

- Be prepared for the worker to be upset or argumentative.
- Do your best not to engage in any acrimony or be sucked into a debate.
- What you say in this encounter could come back to haunt you in a legal setting later on, and wreak havoc for both you and your organization.
- Best to keep a level head and always stick to the books.

The manager also needs to put some time into making sure he's prepared for the task legally. That means checking in with the human resources department to ensure that t's are crossed and i's are dotted. Pay close attention to protocol, and take care to get the language right. Ask an HR supervisor for direction on the employer's obligations in such situations, and to identify if there are any elements about this firing case that make it unique. What your personality data tells you in your Predictive Index will also protect you. If you are a proactive, assertive person with a wee bit of detail, get your ducks in a row in this process.

A "good-enough" mentality

Firing is tough for leaders, as it often signals that we have failed. Better leaders like to lead a great team of happy, engaged and performing employees. When our group, our team, are the right picks and we manage them well from their world, success is more predictable. However, business pressures and whispers or commands from the top to fill open roles sometimes push us to settle.

Often when hiring in the first place, you find yourself with very few candidates to backfill empty positions, so you go with "good-enough" candidates, your B or C players, because it's less hassle than trying to find someone new. So now you've got someone who's not a perfect fit for the role, who isn't as productive as they should be. They're plugging a hole is all. That probably means lowered productivity, people who aren't selling as much. They're only *good enough*. Are we headed for a good-enough economy?

The challenge in this whole sacrificial scene is that service levels suffer. And as service levels continue on a death spiral, AI will replace them.

My doctor is wonderful. He has a high level of detail, is very happy in his job, has good bedside manner, is very high paced, follows the rules and has an altruistic orientation. So he's an example of the right person in the bus. My previous doctor had no detail, gave me seven to ten minutes and didn't know I had celiac disease. Selfishly, I had to let that first doctor go because he was not doing the right work. I cannot have someone who is a C player as my doctor.

Michael Weening, with Calix, in San Jose, California, is a client of ours at Predictive Success. When he was at Salesforce.com and Bell in Canada, he was famous for de-streaming employees. He would create a model for his salespeople — they had to have a high level of assertiveness, a mid-range of detail and be tenacious. Anyone who didn't fit this model wasn't appropriate for the role. He was successful because he put his sales team into roles that allowed them to fit the requirements of what was being asked. Sometimes, he had to have what he called a "necessary ending" that was forced because people didn't like the de-streaming. It was like trimming a rosebush and cutting the bud off. When you put people who don't fit behaviorally into your model, that's where all your drama lies, that's where your absenteeism lies, that's where the butterflies in your stomach are. When it's shared with the employee, it oftentimes leads to an ending, a fair ending, where the staffer gets out of the conflict zone into a role that's better suited to them.

The moment of truth

The old adage "hire slowly, fire quickly" is a sound one. Once the supervisor has scheduled the meeting with his employee (and a rep from another department), equipped himself with data points enough to address the questions that will arise and rehearsed how the scenario might play out, he is ready to enter the fray. It's worth noting that if the person is a virtual employee, the manager needs to enact a face-to-face meeting. The alternative is tantamount to breaking up by text.

The question of when to do the deed is entirely subjective, and different schools of thought offer different wisdom on the subject. Some suggest Friday's the sensible bet, for the opportunity it gives the employee to come to terms with his new reality over the weekend, and also to limit the potential for rage-fueled destruction at the office. A Monday firing, however, offers the staffer a full week of job hunting for replacement employment.

As for the most opportune time of day to let an employee go, there's widespread agreement that morning is best. Practically speaking, that spares the manager the discomfort of a full day's worth of dread. It's also more merciful to the employee, who could otherwise feel duped into a workday that all his superiors knew was going to culminate in his termination. Any work on the individual's docket should be passed off to someone else at pretty much the same moment he's called in to be fired. Needless to say, you should hold the meeting in a private place.

In consultation with HR, prepare a simple, concise script. Keep your language neutral; the less small talk, the better. Begin with the punch line: maybe say, "I have some bad news," or, "I'm sorry to have to be saying this," and then tell them the reason for their termination simply. Maybe they haven't met their sales targets, a shortfall they'd presumably be aware of before the meeting. Or maybe it's more amorphous, like they're not a good personality fit with the rest of the firm. Whatever it is, get to it quickly and explain it succinctly. Experts recommend speaking in the past tense, so the employee understands implicitly that the decision has already been made.

Where appropriate, offer words of gratitude for the employee's service and even for specific tasks they've performed on the company's behalf. And then invite engagement. But do so in a firm posture. As much as it's important for the manager to employ compassion from start to finish in this meeting, he can't let the impulse to downplay its sharp edges get the better of him. This is not, after all, a staff picnic. And our instincts to soften the blow when we have to give someone difficult news are counterintuitive. Taking that tack can muddy the waters and even expose the company to legal liability.

The meeting should be brief and to the point, though all the players need to accommodate the possibility that the employee may need some time to process what she's learning. She will almost certainly need at least a beat to absorb the news, and it behooves her manager to afford her that, with as much empathy as is appropriate. The employee will likely be in a bit of a state of shock and will look to shut down the unpleasant encounter quickly. Plan on spending between fifteen minutes and half an hour in the engagement.

The meeting should close with a verbal explanation of next steps. These include such security-focused details as the return of work files, employee passcards and passwords, and the shutting down of email and access to confidential data. It's essential that these things be arranged with HR and the IT department prior to the termination, lest a furious newly former employee return to his desk bent on inflicting damage. In many offices, it's standard for an HR representative to attend at the desk of the just-terminated employee to physically take receipt of company-issued devices such as electronics and security badges. Often, a severance package doesn't kick in until all company property has been returned. If the employee has medical and dental benefits, this is also the time to explain what happens with those.

Finally, the manager should offer a sincere expression to the departing employee, perhaps of gratitude for the time he's put in, if that's suitable (and it's much more likely to be so in the case of a downsizing than, say, of theft). Wish the employee well, and mean it. Again, if it makes sense, offer the person a reference. If the situation warrants it, extend the generous spirit even further. I've heard of an executive who, at the close of an early-in-the-day termination meeting, offered the employee the opportunity to spend his last day as he pleased. This option extends to the worker the chance to retain his dignity, and makes for a much kinder exodus than simply giving him a box and telling him to pack up and get out. In this case, the dismissed employee spent the day bidding proper farewells to his colleagues and clients, and then went on to become a positive brand ambassador to his company, post-split. Close out the meeting with a sincere handshake.

And make sure to hang around at it until its natural ending. In other words, don't abandon the scene just because it would be easier to bail and leave the closing details to the HR rep. Effective management calls for compassion, and a firing situation puts that dictum to the ultimate test. It's a nice touch for the manager to walk the employee back to his desk and then leave the office with him. This kind of treatment demonstrates humanity.

After the fact: termination is natural, actually

The way a manager handles the post-termination scene is significant to the ongoing well-being of the employees left behind. As much as the dismissal of a worker is a highly private affair between the company and the individual being let go, there's no denying the reach of its impact. After all, the person was part of a corporate community whose members will not only suffer her absence but perhaps be left ill at ease about the security of their own continued employment.

The more mindful the supervisor's approach here, the less damage everyone is exposed to. Indeed, in a perfect world, this unfortunate turn of events can be turned into a growing opportunity for the company. If a manager can reveal himself to be an empathetic soul who was respectful, accessible and responsive in his treatment of the dismissed individual, and if he demonstrated a compassionate regard for the organization's core values, he can shine. And those left in the fired person's wake can gain new respect for the way their manager negotiated the unpleasant incident.

So Job One once the termination has taken place is to share the news with your team. Plan for this in advance, and schedule time with members of the fired worker's department (or, in a smaller organization, the entire company), to get the news on the table.

You don't owe these folks the finer details — they're personal, after all and, besides, it sets an ugly precedent to badmouth a former employee. Nor do you need to defend your position around your decision. Just tell the team broadly what transpired and entertain their questions honestly. Invite their suggestions for how to minimize the impact of the fired employee's absence.

Such a meeting provides a sterling opportunity to express your company's state of mind around the performance of its employees, and to reassure them of their continuance with the company. You might emphasize that the person was fired for cause, and that the organization is not looking to shed roles generally. On the other hand, this event can offer up a natural opportunity for highlighting the company's intolerance for inappropriate behavior.

After, the mindful manager needs to focus on the practical matters around the resulting hole the person's departure creates in the company fabric. Acknowledge that the workload may be higher while the organization maps out a new strategy, but impress upon your staff that you have a plan. It's key to be future-looking at this stage, and to encourage employees' participation in getting back on track. By allowing everyone to engage, you help mitigate what are undoubtedly mixed emotions among the folks left behind.

The ripples from your stone

Consistency is key here, especially as some of the remaining staff may continue to associate with their departing friend. Indeed, it's fair to say that workplaces are very often roiling pits of social engagement. In other words, people tend to develop friendships with their fellow employees. And that's a good thing. Statistics demonstrate that when employees have a pal at work, they are much likelier to stay than they would in a company of workmates only. According to a study in the *Journal of Business and*

Psychology, workers report higher job satisfaction when they feel they have even the *opportunity* for friendship. A 2013 survey of 2,223 business people across Australia, meanwhile, found that 67 percent of workers with the intention of staying in their current job counted "good relationship with co-workers" as the major reason. That's above "job satisfaction" (63 percent), "flexible working arrangements" (57 percent) and even salary (which ranked seventh, at 46 percent). So when someone's friend gets fired, the results can have truly damaging ramifications for more than just the individual clearing out his desk.

And you need to think beyond the immediate friend circle too. Indeed, there's no accounting for the people with whom your recently excised staffer might come into contact. It's a fair guess that this individual will stay at least peripherally in the same industry whence they came — your industry — and so it stands to reason that the cast of characters with whom he interacts will include some of the same players. These might be customers, suppliers or employees, of the past, present or future persuasion. You simply never know where this person is going to land.

When I was at Microsoft, they were mindful of this when they created an alumni network. It was not restricted to employees who had left the company of their own volition; those who had been nudged out the door by others were welcome too. That inclusiveness is meaningful in its cognizance of the varying scenarios that might deliver a person to this group. There's a message here about the need for managers to keep things decent and respectful in their acts of termination. Microsoft's extension of this past-workers arrangement is not a unique phenomenon either. Accenture, Cisco and Salesforce.com have similar alumni organizations for their ex-employees.

And the ripples go further still. A swift, respectful termination that doesn't burn any bridges mitigates the likelihood of being flamed on Glassdoor. Glassdoor is one of the fastest-growing job and recruitment databases. Here, curious job sniffers will find company reviews, CEO approval ratings, salary reports, interview reviews and questions, benefits reviews, office photos and more. A former employee who was let go disrespectfully is considerably more likely to go to this site and burn their old company than one who was handled well in his letting-go. So you want to be as fair to these individuals on the way out as you were on the way in.

While agonizing about how to handle a looming obligation to fire someone, it's good for a manager to keep the following truth high in mind: this task is as much a favor to the individual as it is a blow. You're letting them go, after all, because they weren't a good fit for the role and/or the company. By doing so, you are also setting them free. If an employee in a sales role isn't hitting her targets, you're depriving her of the opportunity to do so — and to enjoy the personal satisfaction that comes with it — by sustaining the status quo. With the termination, you're giving her a new path forward. The alternative is to keep her hostage, facilitating an ongoing drain on her productivity.

Chapter 5

How to Mindfully Handle the Post-Termination

"Being fired has some of the advantages of dying without its supreme disadvantages. People say extra-nice things about you, and you get to hear them."

— HOWARD ZINN

Statistics Canada estimates that, in 2015, around 158,400 Canadians between the ages of fifty-five and sixty-four were handed pink slips. That's a lot of people to suddenly find themselves without the comfort and security of employment. But such is the current plight of older workers in corporate North America, where getting laid off is a very real and ongoing possibility for a big chunk of the population. It's the pits to get the boot at any stage in life, but to experience this loss in the latter years of one's professional livelihood, after one has presumably established a reputation and some kind of legacy of expertise, well, that's a serious downer. In that case, from the employee's perspective it doesn't feel like being set free. Imagine the pain when the employee has been with the firm for many years.

Recently, my former book publisher, Wiley, terminated their SVP of sales. The boss is a wonderful person with twenty-seven years of service, and is as dedicated an employee as I have ever coached and worked with. She was trained in analytics and was a great Predictive Index analyst. However, the book publishing world is going through dramatic change. The way higher-education books are presented and sold is evolving and the margins are being challenged. This was unfortunate for my former coach, and being let go was hurtful. Her entire world was leading the North American sales team. They loved her and still do. This was a tough transition for all, but I am sure she will land well in the months ahead. The challenge for Wiley will be to move the sales team in the new direction they believe they need to go, and to do this they decided they need a fresh, new approach. Time will tell. And for bosses, the scene is further challenged by the requirement to pull off a successful follow-up.

Along with divorce and moving house, being dismissed from a job is among the most stressful life events a person can suffer. No sugar-coating this one: getting fired sucks, especially if it's from work you enjoyed. In an instant, your daily routines are shot out of the water, and you find yourself still in pajamas at 3 p.m., binge-watching *Bob's Burgers* and creeping your ex-colleagues on social media. But, for lots of reasons, it's critical to manage this blow to the plexus not with kicks and complaints but in a state of grace and mindfulness. When you've been let go, it's good for your soul not to fill it with bitterness. And an upbeat mind frame can only serve a person well as he launches himself into the job-hunting ether. Positivity attracts positivity, after all.

Still, anyone who tells you that maintaining a sense of breezy optimism after getting whacked is a cinch simply isn't being truthful. It's a genuine slog to be gracious and thoughtful in the face of such a gut-wallop. And pulling it off calls for a serious psychological commitment to mindful optimism and good cheer.

The numbers

If you're laid off at age fifty-five, you've still got at least five years of personal industry to put in before you can claim a government pension, so finding a professional replacement is kind of essential. But fresh employment is hard to find when you're near the end of what's deemed to be a person's conventional employable period. In the twenty-eight-year "longitudinal worker" study Statistics Canada conducted on older workers seeking re-employment in 2014, just 62.9 percent of men and 57.2 percent of women aged fifty-five to fifty-nine were successful in finding jobs to replace the ones they lost. And for folks in the next five-year bracket (sixty to sixty-four), the numbers were even lower, with just 46.8 percent of men and 41.3 percent of women landing new jobs.

Most older workers who did find further employment did so within the first year after being laid off (and 15.5 percent of these over-fifty-five men and 11.2 percent of these over-fifty-five women skipped among multiple jobs). If they didn't, their likelihood of ever getting a job shrank meaningfully. We will continue to see layoffs as companies transition in the new world economy.

Things are no brighter south of the border, where eBay announced in 2018 that it will be cutting a single-digit percentage of jobs. The company currently employs 14,100 people. General Mills terminated 625 of its 38,000 employees in 2018. Even tech leader Tesla, the automobile company, cut 9 percent of its workforce in 2018.

The bad-firing example

People hate change — some personalities more than others. It's in the post-whack scenario that you really see this. One of the worst cases of a post-whack fiasco I ever saw was my former boss at Microsoft. This guy was very assertive, had lots of energy, had a very high level of tenaciousness and persuasiveness, and didn't get stuck in the details. When he was let go from the enterprise partner group, they paraded him out with security in front of his secretary and his team. That was a classic example of how not to whack. It should've been done privately, and with a high level of persuasiveness and collaboration. Because of his need to connect with others, he had strong relationships with people, and when those relationships were shattered by security walking him out with HR, it rattled the levels below him.

There was a mass exodus at Microsoft subsequently because of the way that leader was whacked. When packages are given to people who are not assertive, are slow to trust, are very sequential or like lots of detail, you must be mindful: Change is the enemy for that profile, and they would absolutely have to be handled privately and followed up with a long career-training stretch. That personality absolutely has to be considered when you're giving someone a package.

We like to think that when we show respect to the individual and treat them well on the way out, it sends a great signal to whoever's coming in. If you base your treatment on their personality, it's objective and humane.

We're doing some work with the CIBC, which is moving 15,000 employees into the same building. Bankers, loan adjudicators and the like are all about risk protection and fighting change. So moving roles or getting packaged is enormously stressful for them. They don't like it and resist it. All their life they've been fighting it, and now it's being forced upon them. These are the people who need to be handled with kid gloves. Again, analytics can assist here. Where will the sales team need to be? How will they have their team huddles? Who will need to collaborate with whom to be able to lead and close projects on time and on budget?

Coming to terms

There's no shame in admitting that you kind of define yourself by what you do for a living. You are a teacher, a financial analyst, the head of sales at a software company, an architect. It's the first thing your brain scares up when summoned to lay claim to a definition for your person. And then, one day, a day on the heels of your dismissal from your job, you come up short. What are you, after all, if you're not the profession that's preoccupied you for the better part of your adult life?

This is where you need to learn to love the person that *is*, not the person that *does*. To realize that you're not a human *doing*, you're a human *being*. Always a good idea to get all your reliable and science-based insights on your own "blind spots," your potential break points, and learn to leverage these for your own path forward.

But more on the mindful piece later. First, it's got to be heartening to realize how common it is to be in this position. There's comfort in numbers, after all, and a conversation about getting laid off is going to attract a lot of I've-been-there-too hits.

In a typical group, say some stats, as many as two-thirds of the assemblage has been fired at some time in their life. In the United States, an average of 55,939 employees were laid off or fired from their jobs every single day (including weekends and holidays) in 2014. According to the Bureau of Labor Statistics, the typical American goes through ten different jobs before reaching forty. That makes for a lot of people wandering about, trying to fill their hours, suddenly without the key descriptor that for so long summed up their raisons d'être.

And there are some prominent folks in this club too. Steve Jobs was fired from his first post at Apple, remember. And Anna Wintour was canned from an editorial role at *Harper's Bazaar*. Indeed, Ms. Wintour would later go on to recommend the experience. "Everyone should be sacked at least once in their career because perfection doesn't exist," she told author Alastair Campbell for his book *Winners: And How They Succeed*. "It's important to have setbacks, because that is the reality of life."

The reasons people have these setbacks thrust upon them vary wildly. Could be the employee suffered a personality conflict with his manager. Maybe he simply couldn't get the hang of the job. Or perhaps it's that his company had to cut part of its workforce in order to continue to exist, and he fell square in the camp on the other side of the blade. In any case, it's important to remember that these things happen. And that you are not alone.

Up from the ashes

The steps that follow a dismissal are significant ones. They set the stage for the next chapter of life. And there's no question: an individual who is able to recover from this tectonic shift gracefully and mindfully will fare better than someone who lets it crush him.

When Andrew Mason was fired from his post as CEO of Groupon, he projected a positive outlook from the get-go. In a public letter after the sack, he told the world that he loved Groupon and was terribly proud of what he'd helped create there. "I'm OK with having failed at this part of the journey," he said. "If Groupon was Battletoads, it would be like I made it all the way to the Terra Tubes without dying on my first ever play through. I am so lucky to have had the opportunity to take the company this far with all of you."

Here's how to similarly land on the right side of the divide.

Take care

Having a healthy, peaceful mindset is an important step in surfacing from this setback. Everyone has their own tricks for achieving this.

Employing a regimen of good self-care that includes exercising and journaling can help. Maybe meditation will be of assistance to you at this stage. Talk to friends and family and make yourself available to their advice and comfort. If necessary, seek some outside help and enlist a counselor.

Assume responsibility

Only those workers whose corporate dismissals were purely the result of a downsizing or complete company dissolution can even consider exempting themselves from this step in the recovery process. It behooves everyone else to acknowledge their own role in the demise of their employment with their organization. The alternative — e.g., imagining that a pack of bad guys treated you poorly and that you were nothing but a victim to their whims — will do nothing to speed your ascent to a better place. No matter the specifics of your job and your dismissal, there's little doubt that you played some part in what transpired.

Groupon's Mason was entirely cool with his ownership of blame when he was fired. The company simply wasn't thriving under his watch, and he acknowledged that. Its stocks were falling, and competition was exploding. Groupon's employees, he said, deserved better. What a gracious response to this turn of events.

And hand in hand with accepting your culpability is defining it. Here's where you need a great big dose of psychological backbone. This is the facing-your-demons stuff they harp on about. Think long and hard about what you did wrong in this position and wrap your mind around its sharp edges and dark recesses. Did you fail to discharge all the duties of your post? Were you a source of conflict in the office? Did you mess up? Name your sins. Then move forward.

Don't burn bridges

Next comes the business of taking your leave from your former company with dignity. No matter the thorny particulars that surround your departure, how you physically depart your post can affect your success down the line. While a receiving line of earnest farewells to your suddenly former workmates might seem a more compassionate alternative to simply disappearing from their midst with no explanation, that kind of thing can be pretty awkward. Better to say your goodbyes selectively (even better, electronically) and slip away without fanfare.

Don't pilfer office supplies or make a public fuss in your departure. It's important that you keep your negative feelings about the firing, the company and the employees within it under wraps. You never know when you might need a reference, or even if your job might open up again if the company goes through a restructuring in coming months. If you pitched a fit in the lobby on your last day or erased critical corporate documents from the server, you might not be in the running. Better to always behave in a dignified fashion.

As Jeff Cohen says in his book *The Complete Idiot's Guide to Recession-Proof Careers*, "that small sense of satisfaction from dissing a former company will ultimately be outweighed if it costs you a future job." If nothing else, a cheerful mindset promotes good karma.

Be forward-looking

So you tanked, and now your tenure at your old company is in your rearview mirror. Too bad. But what's out there beyond your windshield? By focusing on what you're going to do next and how you're going to find another job, you necessarily distract your mind from the past and launch it into the future. That kind of head-up attitude does wonders, too, to tamp down your feelings of anger, sadness and frustration, nudging you into a mental space that's much more attractive to hiring committees.

Seeking your next post

When you've sufficiently recovered from your experience that you can imagine making a practical advancement toward your life's next spectacular turn round the wheel, that's when you should start looking for other work. That's a big deal, reaching that psychological milestone, and it needs to be tackled without haste. Dash off a few cover letters and send out some CVs the very afternoon you feel you can. Shed the PJs and write a LinkedIn entry.

Get out all the analytic reports you can on your DNA. It is a wonderful time for reflection. A whitespace time for you to really study who you are, your blind spots, your strengths. Take the time to complete great personality tests and surveys like the Predictive Index (see www.predictivesuccess.com/request-a-demo), the Myers–Briggs (my-personality-test.com/personality-type-indicator), the Grit test data score (angeladuckworth.com/grit-scale) and the CliftonStrengths assessment, formerly StrengthsFinder (www.gallupstrength-scenter.com). Maybe even start your own website to promote your undeniable employability.

Some employment strategists suggest writing down every place you've ever wanted to work and doing at least five things a day to advance you in that dream-job direction. You might engage the services of a career coach at this stage. Such a professional can help you identify your past accomplishments and rebrand yourself for your next foray into the job market.

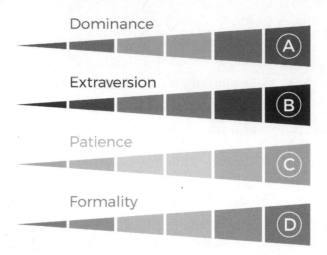

Dominance (A)

Extraversion (B)

Patience (C)

Formality (D)

Source: the Predictive Index®, a registered trademark of Predictive Index LLC and used here with permission.

The elephant in the room

When you do start casting about for your next gig, and when you score an interview with a potential employer, you need to be mindful of their interest in your professional past. In other words, you can be pretty sure you're going to be asked the question: "Why did you leave your last job?" You do yourself a significant favor to be prepared with a response to it.

Plan One would be to preempt this eventuality with an unsolicited declaration to your prospective new bosses that you were fired from your last post, before they even have a chance to ask. The philosophy here is that you'll look more honorable than if you shrink back into a corner and present a front of sniveling ignorance about the question everyone in the room knows needs to be leveled. (Though this approach doesn't mean you waltz right into the interview room and announce that you were canned from your last post; it's never cool to lead with the negative.)

There are at least a couple of schools of thought on Plan Two — the plan that sees you not volunteering information about the demise of your last job but not shirking from addressing it either. In *Job Interviews for Dummies*, Joyce Lain Kennedy suggests answering the interrogators' question about what happened squarely and without hesitation. "Keep it brief, keep it honest and keep it moving," she recommends. If you can legitimately say the development was not your fault, do. Maybe it's entirely accurate to say the new boss wanted to bring in his own team. Or maybe it's fair to simply say it was "not a good fit."

Otherwise, straightforwardly explain that you've benefitted in some way from the experience. Say, "I've learned everything I can from that position, and I'm looking for new opportunities where I can learn and grow." You might even offer a specific illustration of how you've transformed the negative into a positive.

The truth always outs

Always be truthful in your dealings with prospective employers. If you lie or contradict yourself in any way, you can bet you'll be found out. By sticking to one story — the accurate one — you save yourself the trouble of keeping track of your lines (to say nothing of your lies). And it's much less stressful.

Only good-mouth, no gossip, ever . . .

Never disparage your former manager or company to a prospective employer. Even if they treated you abysmally and turfed you without any regard for your dignity or service, you must demonstrate unwavering respect in all of your references to them. Perhaps the new company for which you are interviewing has some experience with your former comrades, and its people will know without your saying a word that you've just come out of a genuinely miserable experience. If that's the case, your noble display of restraint will look good on you. And if the suits on the other side of the desk have no idea what you've suffered, well, at least by withholding your horror stories you won't look like a sour-grapes ingrate who hasn't accepted his fate with grace.

Fake it till you make it

You would be clever to take this interview strategy out for a test run or two, and practice your script with someone posing as the interviewer. The more mindfully you embrace the reality of your situation in the face of a job prospect, the more confidently you'll be able to address it. Encourage a role-playing friend or significant other to be brutal with their line of questioning, and to cast a wide net of inquiry that imagines every scenario.

The post-termination positives

At the end of the day, your intention is to convince future employers that the job loss in your recent past was but an anomalous blip from which you've not only recovered but usefully evolved. While the topic will almost certainly come up and demand attention, once addressed, the focus needs to shift to the viability of your candidacy for this position and your eminent capacity to do the work. That means presenting a persona that is confident, calm and mindful.

Emerging from a job-loss situation with one's head held high isn't for the faint of heart. It calls for forbearance, fortitude and a fierce commitment to a mindful plan to come out the other side a winner. Losing your job, even at a late professional stage in life, isn't a tragedy. Indeed, it's not a huge stretch to cast it as a rare opportunity for a restart. Like so much in life, how you handle it is all about the mindset. People remember you as a leader for how you made them "feel." In a job-market era where you as the leader have your own "boss brand," you need to own it, manage it and continue to evolve. Your "boss brand" ought to create a job destination.

Chapter 6

The Mindfulness of Applying Science to Decision-Making

"The difficulty lies not so much in developing new ideas as in escaping from old ones."

— J. M. KEYNES

Long, long gone are the days when a CEO or hiring manager would extend an offer of employment to the boss's kid's buddy, say. Or would make a professional deployment decision on the strength of some vague commentary uncovered in stacks of static reports, spreadsheets or binders. Today's scene is an immeasurably more sophisticated one. Thank goodness.

It is also loaded with challenges. Corporate leaders need help to effectively manage today's diverse workforce like never before. And the nuanced understanding of people for which this task calls can only be achieved with a comprehensive plundering of analytics. The data are there. The modern HR leader has a whack of resources just waiting for her effective leveraging in aid of increasing worker productivity and job satisfaction. Indeed, today's crop of managers has access to more smart, on demand, real-time information around recruitment, employee engagement, retention, leadership development, redeployment and retirement than ever before.

And the pile is still growing.

Time to dive in.

Why wouldn't you? By utilizing the full complement of objective workplace data that's on offer through thoughtful analytics testing, leaders can implement spot-on workforce plans that set their organizations up for enduring success. This rich store helps a manager make all of those decisions she stares down every day (who to hire, who to fire, who to promote, who to encourage, who to discourage and so on). It can be applied to maximizing staffers' efficiency, productivity and profit. And it makes the lots of these workers more satisfying through its ability to matchmake talents and interests with personnel requirements. Assessments such as The Predictive Index Behavioral Assessment™ offer assurance that employees' behaviors and values are in alignment with both a company's current culture and its plans for the future. There's nothing like having the right number of people, with the right skills, in the right places, at the right time, to boost workplace morale.

The early days of data maximization

But the business of applying science to decision-making is still in its infancy. Although companies collect a great deal of data about their employees, most of them don't do a very good job of taking advantage of it for insight. And as much as HR professionals are trained to develop talent, enhance culture and increase engagement, it seems that they're flagging in their grasp of data science and its potential for their organizations' well-being. According to Accenture's 2016 outlook *How Well Do You Know Your Workforce?*, "Many companies are struggling just to get basic reporting right. They may not even know exactly how many people work for them, in what jobs and in what regions. And many still rely on first-generation spreadsheets to manage HR data."

In the February 16, 2017, *Globe and Mail*, Debbie McGrath, CEO of HR.com, lamented that the HR departments of more Canadian firms aren't exploiting the data available to them and developing evidence-based strategies around them. "We have companies that are global leaders in workplace analytics," she told reporter Mary McIninch, "yet they derive the majority of their revenue helping companies outside Canada."

The largest HR association in North America, the Society for Human Resource Management (SHRM) Foundation, believes that analytics are about to explode in HR. According to the SHRM's 2016 report, *Shaping the Future of HR* (researched by the Economist Intelligence Unit), 82 percent of organizations planned to begin using or enhance their existing use of talent-related big data over the subsequent three years.

According to Bersin by Deloitte's 2017 High-Impact People Analytics research, only 2 percent of surveyed organizations are "highly mature" in people analytics. On Deloitte's *Capital H* blog, contributor Kathi Enderes predicted that "people analytics will become a principal supporting factor in the

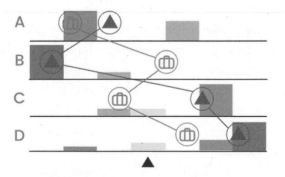

Group analytic map: top performers vs. future requirement, general manager role, large national retailer, 2017 study.

Source: the Predictive Index®, a registered trademark of Predictive Index LLC and used here with permission.

growing productivity . . . of the individual, empowering each person with the insights to help them do their best work." This is a powerful potential accelerator for leaders.

Dissecting decision-making

Before anyone can fully appreciate the power and potential of mindfully applying science to decision-making, they need to first understand the mechanics of the process.

A slew of digital sources insist that human beings make some 35,000 conscious decisions a day (or at least an adult human being does; a child makes closer to 3,000). From determining what shoes to wear to which person to marry, we are constantly in the throes of selecting from among our options. Indeed, researchers at Cornell University declare that we make 226.7 decisions each day about food alone! (Consider the number of sandwiches a person contemplates in a lifetime!) For individuals operating inside a corporate environment, the decision count is exponentially higher. No wonder *Vogue* editor Anna Wintour calls decisiveness the most important quality a leader can have.

Still, for all the burden of expectation decision-making delivers to our daily toil, the exercise is not a drawn-out one. It takes just a split second to make a decision. Ask Malcolm Gladwell, who wrote a 296-page book on the subject. In *Blink*, the Canadian author's landmark bestseller, Gladwell reveals that the greatest decision-makers aren't the people who can wade through the most information or devote the most time to deliberating their particulars, but the people who've perfected the art of "thin-slicing."

A term bandied about by philosophers and psychologists alike, "thin-slicing" refers to a person's ability to find patterns in events based merely on narrow segments of experience and then to make an inference from this modicum of data about a larger situation. Judgments made according to thin-slicing, say the experts, can be every bit as accurate as those made based on much more information.

Ultimately, though, the secret to succeeding at decision-making is recognizing that it's an imperfect science. You're going to sometimes make the right choice, but you're also going to make some big, ugly, flaming wrong ones. A person's ability to react to these missteps swiftly, nimbly and mindfully — and to be comfortable with the idea of failing — is key. By anticipating the worst, you can find the courage to dive into the decision's deepest end.

Finally, don't overload the decision-making enterprise with the input of too many participants. It stands to reason that the more people that there are involved in coming to a conclusion, the more labored the process will be. The dozen-member jury construct notwithstanding, decision-making teams of fewer than twelve people are probably the most effective.

Why you need to leverage big data at work

All right. Now that we understand the role of decision-making in our daily lives, and the mechanics behind its machinations, it's time to think about how this subject fits into a professional environment. Depending upon its access to data-gathering resources, the modern organization today could potentially find itself swimming in more details than it could ever put to effective use. Enter the art of data management, and its power to make the unmanageable manageable.

Every sizable business stands to benefit from the use of basic, time-tested data analytics throughout the organization. No doubt this still-emerging specialty has much to offer workplaces hungry for the shortest line from A to B. It's why managers need to craft a smart philosophy around big-data management. Otherwise, the corporate mysteries with which they're besieged won't ever get solved. Among those corporate mysteries, consider why the best employees are leaving their organization, and why some staffers are more productive or creative than others. And why are employers paying through the teeth for bad hires?

There's a slew of data out there on the cost of hiring someone who's a bad fit for the role or company. Think you can sidestep it? Think again. While you might be able to hold out for a bit with these rough picks, the rubber will eventually hit the road, and you'll have to release them to the universe. And all of the financial and temporal investment you've put into onboarding these employees into your organization? For naught.

You might as well have held a match to a stash of cash.

Exactly how much you've burned is a matter of some debate, but there's lots of research that attempts to assign a value to it. In a survey completed by CareerBuilder, 25 percent of companies said that one bad hire had cost them a minimum of $50,000. In another assessment, this across a randomly selected group of seven Canadian companies from diverse industries, personnel costs were revealed to average 44 percent of total expenses and 36 percent of total revenue.

How do you leverage big data at work?

There are a few pieces of sound advice managers would do well to heed in crafting their big-data management philosophy.

For one, it's a good idea to launch the proceedings by talking to an expert. The HR side of the coin might be flagging in its appreciation for — or at least grasp of — the powers of workplace analytics, but there are some folks who are bona fide authorities in this field. Rather than suffering the learning curve in a steep solo effort, companies should seek out these experts and retain their services in the early days and then in onboarding their staff in the essentials.

Similarly, it is the responsibility of a clever corporate leader to identify someone within his own organization who can champion this effort on the home front. An employee who's fired up about the potential of big data can meaningfully advance his peers' embrace of this unfamiliar new concept. Having identified a couple of big-data champions, both in-house and out, managers do themselves the next big favor by being specific about their goals for leveraging the data these designated helpers will assist in uncovering. By aligning the material with your objectives, you can ensure that you employ it to best effect. And don't forget the essential humanity at the heart of this subject. As intimidating as all the numbers might be, the mindful manager understands that this business is ultimately about people.

Optimizing your data

Getting the most out of the information available to you is a matter of knuckling down on a few elements.

For one, you'll want to ensure the quality of your data is at its highest. There's questionable value to data that wasn't collected in a reliable, validated way. That means addressing the comprehensiveness and rigor of your data-seeking initiatives. It also means revisiting the specifics of your inquiries. Poll staffers to get a feel for what preoccupies them, and dig into it with your survey questions.

It's also smart to introduce a layer of structure to your data-collecting efforts. And to convey a harder-line sense of expectation around managers' participation in them.

From there, it's all about the analysis. This final step, of course, is all about sorting, managing, scrutinizing and leveraging your data. Job One here is to ensure that you have expertise available to you — whether in-house or contracted out — for conducting the necessary analysis.

Appointing a CDO (chief data officer)

A while back, research and advisory company Gartner estimated that 90 percent of large organizations will have a Chief Data Officer by 2019. This development is powering business leaders' appreciation for the huge potential of digital business analytics. Creating an executive position to oversee them seems the next logical step.

Gartner also acknowledged the steep learning curve that'll accompany this development and predicted that just half of these new CDOs would be successful by the end of 2019. It offered these six tips for a brand-new CDO to successfully create an information strategy with relevant metrics that tie the activities of a team to measurable business outcomes:

- Create an enterprise information management strategy based on the organization's business strategy and predominant value discipline.
- Work tirelessly to build trust with various business stakeholders, especially the CIO.
- Educate senior leaders and peers about the role that data and information play in overall business success.
- Establish baselines on information governance and data monetization from which progress can be measured.
- Tie quantifiable information metrics to quantifiable business key performance indicators to demonstrate tangible success.
- Adopt formal information asset measures and share them with the organization.

Hiring for the job

In the past, the best we could conjure was a loose assessment of a potential employee's smarts, courtesy of an IQ test. But as much as this hoary tool of segregation has a reputation for predicting work performance (research shows that IQ tests do that at least as well as competency interviews do and about ten times better than personality tests), the IQ test is desperately flawed. After all, this examination of academic proficiency measures only those cognitive skills that are key to *scholastic success*, not success in business. (When Alfred Binet was commissioned to create a measure of academic intelligence more than a century ago, he based his model on identifying which cognitive skills determined a student's aptitude for mastering a selection of school subjects.)

Cognitive test questions don't assess the practical, on-your-feet thinking skills needed in business. And these tests have been repeatedly accused of racial and gender bias. At the end of the day, what do they have to say of critical thinking? Or how well someone works with others?

Cognitive ability tests typically use questions or pose word problems that are designed to measure a person's ability to learn quickly and their facilities for the art of logic, reasoning, reading comprehension and other enduring mental abilities that are fundamental to success in many different jobs.

These tests also assess a person's aptitude or potential to solve job-related problems by providing information about their mental abilities, such as verbal or mathematical reasoning and perceptual abilities like speed in recognizing letters of the alphabet.

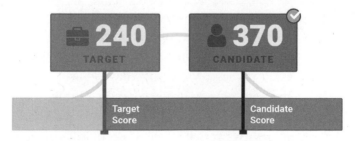

By measuring candidate cognitive score against a baseline, organizations can understand the time a new hire will take to get up to speed.
The Predictive Index® is a registered trademark of Predictive Index LLC and is used here with permission.

A person's acumen in vocabulary, arithmetic and spatial reasoning amount to almost nothing when it comes to their skills as a manager. Individuals with extensive professional experience could even be insulted by the overly academic and elementary line of questioning these tests tend to embrace.

Ideally, rather than concentrating on academic subjects and specific industry expertise or experience, behavioral assessment tools should focus on the particular cognitive subjects associated with executive work. Namely: accomplishing tasks, working with others, enduring self-criticism, processing power.

The performance-review piece

Performance reviews are similarly flawed. First used by the US Army in World War I to weed out the chaff, and called back into service in World War II to target high achievers, they had outgrown much of their usefulness by the 1960s. Organizations flattened, managers felt crushed by data and expectations around its followup application, and eventually companies abandoned the practice. In 2011, Kelly Services was the first big firm to officially drop performance reviews. Adobe came next, and other organizations have been shedding their allegiance to this convention ever since.

General Electric now has an app for people to make on-demand comments in real time right after meetings. Relationship audits are always a good thing. The old-fashioned year-end review is seldom anything other than an assessment of the stuff that's been bothering a leader in the previous sixty days — whatever he can dredge up from his liver. As far as I'm concerned, fresh, actionable leadership content should happen each and every week.

Performance reviews are a big topic. Lots of folks out there are currently turning its relevancy around in their brains — some have been for years. Because as much as the basic idea makes sense — the impulse to peg employees along a continuum in terms of their performance, and to watch their progress along that band by way of ongoing comparison — the systems and processes for tracking have become complicated (to execute) and confusing (to justify). While we may all agree on what's important, we don't in terms of what criteria should carry the most weight. Certain confusion is the result. People don't really know where they stand, and when they get passed over for an opportunity, it can have adverse effects.

But the biggest beef about performance reviews is that they fail to deliver the clear, consistent, ongoing feedback that today's employees want. How could a once-a-year affair, begrudgingly approached by all, do that? And the supposition motivating performance reviews' persistence — that people who are motivated by a real desire to learn would respond well to getting critical feedback in a performance review — has backfired. Those individuals who like to learn — presumably some of the best employees — were significantly bothered by the negative feedback they received. In the *Journal of Personnel Psychology*, researchers from Texas A&M University, having tested the effect of goal orientation on individuals' reactions to performance appraisals, wrote that "it seems, contrary to our expectations, that high-learning-goal-orientation individuals are not necessarily appreciative of all types of feedback."

No wonder 70 percent of companies are reconsidering their strategy around performance reviews (says a recent study by research firm Bersin by Deloitte), including consulting firms Deloitte and Accenture, global health services bigwig Cigna, and even GE — the company that popularized the idea of forcing people into a performance curve.

That, say those with their eye on the subject, is because of four things: the changing nature of work, the need for better collaboration, the need to retain top talent and the development cycle of employees.

A better approach would be to coach your employees weekly. If a leader cannot sit down face to face with each person on his team, if he cannot fit them all in each week, then he has too many direct reports to make an impact on them.

The data you collect

One key decision-making exercise for which data has historically been collected is employee engagement. The more engaged your employees are, the more productive they are, the more content they are — this is well understood. So, too, should be the appreciation that this is an area particularly worth your mindful science-based decision-making powers.

Since time immemorial, business leaders have sought to determine their workers' level of satisfaction by conducting surveys. And, for a long time, these were considered the gold standard in assessing employees' feelings about their professional situations and the success that flows from an affirmative consensus. Through employee satisfaction surveys, employers could understand what changes needed to be made to improve their staffers' sense of engagement with the firm.

It hasn't, however, always worked out that way. The credibility of these surveys has long been in dispute. One study — completed by Impact Achievement Group and HRmarketer — found that 48 percent of respondents "did not believe employee surveys provide an honest and accurate assessment." More than that, the study uncovered that "58 percent of respondents agreed that results did not help — or only slightly helped — managers gain a better understanding of what behaviors or practices they could change to improve."

That, say some employee-assessment critics, is because companies are performing evaluations of a particular facet of an employee's professional experience while the employee's focus is on an altogether different facet. In other words, think social media and smartphones. Don't be formal if your employees' lives are informal. *Inc.* magazine suggests approaching employee evaluations from a practical, personal atmosphere. A lunch meeting, on the company's tab? The bottom line is this: the only way to gauge your own employees is to know where they're coming from.

People analytics

More recently recognized for quantifying and improving employee engagement of late is the use of people analytics. Google's corporate headquarters demonstrated the power of this idea in an application to figure out if managers actually make any difference in their subordinates' productivity levels. Managers who received positive feedback and performance ratings, as it turned out, led teams that had high productivity ratings and were highly engaged. Next, Google employed people analytics to identify the major characteristics of a great manager. Today, the massive organization uses the "top eight management behaviors" to identify and develop leaders within the organization.

People analytics is a superstar among decision-making employment tools for its ability to help a company identify and develop its high-potential talent into great leaders. As Google did, companies can use the tools to single out the personality characteristics that are common among their top leaders and use them to devise a behavior profile of the ideal leader.

A piece for *Harvard Business Review* digs into available data to uncover the personality traits shared by such successful CEOs as Elon Musk and Steve Jobs. Dean Stamoulis and his team at executive search firm Russell Reynolds Associates analyzed the profiles of 200 CEOs from around the world. They created an in-depth personality profile for each that analyzed everything from leadership, communication and decision-making styles to interpersonal skills and emotional factors.

While the data revealed that successful CEOs had greater comfort with taking risks, extraversion was not a key quality.

Neither was a tendency to self-promote. In fact, the three key personality traits that this research uncovered were these surprises: a sense of purpose and mission, an ability to zero in on core issues and an acceptance of one's weaknesses.

Without people analytics, we would never have known.

Pre-employment testing is another fertile ground for the application of smart decision-making tactics. Companies use these tests to find the best candidates for a job. These valid, reliable analyses can include the testing of cognitive abilities, knowledge, work skills, physical and motor abilities, personality, emotional intelligence, language proficiency and even integrity. Drug testing can also be utilized as part of the pre-employment process. According to a survey by the American Management Association, "Almost 90 percent of firms that test job applicants say they will not hire job seekers when pre-employment testing finds them to be deficient in basic skills."

Administered correctly, pre-employment testing can help companies save time and cost in the selection process, decrease turnover, increase productivity and improve morale. Even though screening tests are occasionally challenged in court, companies can reduce their legal exposure by making sure that the tests they choose to use don't discriminate against minorities or protected groups and by consistently applying the tests to all candidates.

Service Canada's government website on hiring suggests:

> Historically, employers depend upon résumés, references and interviews to select good employees. In practice, these sources have proved inadequate for the job. While pre-employment assessments are widely available, they have yet to be adopted by the majority of firms in Canada. One of the major reasons for this is that most companies lack an understanding of what pre-employment assessments are and why they are

effective. A pre-employment assessment is a battery of tests used to collect information from job applicants for the purpose of aiding hiring decisions. Such assessments may include items on topics such as motives, ethics, traits, work experience, intelligence, skills, preferences, and preferred work hours. When effectively measured, all of these things may be used, in some capacity, to make accurate predictions about which applicant will perform well on the job and/or which ones will remain with the company.

Use assessment results effectively and consistently. Finally, make sure you are provided adequate training so that you or your hiring managers can effectively and consistently interpret the assessment findings. This is essential so that hiring decisions are made on a consistent and equitable basis. All individuals making hiring decisions should have access to the same information on all candidates. If you have questions or concerns, put a call in to your test vendor for clarification. The high stakes involved in hiring decisions demand that it be done correctly. When pre-employment assessments are used properly, they offer a fair and unbiased selection system that benefits everyone. The company prospers as a result of more productive, reliable and honest employees. Applicants can benefit through increased job satisfaction due to an improved fit to their job." (Source: www.emploisetc.gc.ca.)

Business leaders are forever on the hunt for deep insight into their markets and customers. They have access to truly massive amounts of data and need to use it in a way that lets them frame and solve problems effectively. But in business, this kind of insight alone isn't enough. Companies must use data to make better decisions.

One of the stumbling blocks on the road to big data is the "overwhelmed factor." What data do I need to pay attention to? From my experience, most senior leaders are not going to read that forty-to-fifty-page report on personality for one employee. Academics rarely make good business leaders. However, science leaves a roadmap in its wake. Best boss/leaders love the insights found along it, and the evidence of who was successful in the past for what it tells them about who might be successful in the future. When a whole lot of details are swirling around a person, our instinct is to default to our gut rather than to actual observable things. I don't need big data, the boss might shrug. I know my sales team!

But that head-in-the-sand approach eschews a whole host of available insight. And a mindful manager would never behave in this manner. Finding the right approach in your own company or unit is one of the great challenges in applying data and analytics today. Prioritizing your resource allocation and clarifying your desired outcomes are key.

Chapter 7

The Mindfulness of Incentives and Rewards

"There are two things people want more than sex and money — recognition and praise."

— MARY KAY ASH

It ain't no secret that dangling a prize — or at least the promise of a prize — in front of someone can do plenty to motivate them into action. Performing for recognition and results is tons more satisfying than performing in a void. No kidding.

That's why hundreds of generations of employers ago, someone in upper management signed on to the concept of employee incentives. An incentive program is a formal scheme whereby something of value — sometimes monetary, sometimes not — is extended with the expectation of inspiring a certain behavior in its beneficiary. At its heart, it's a tradeoff. The incentive-offerer gets a productive effort from the recipient, and the recipient gets a trophy. In a perfect world, when the transaction has taken place, employees who are recognized for some stellar aspect of performance gain increased morale, job satisfaction and engagement with organizational functions, and employers gain a workplace that's enhanced by increased efficiency, boosted sales and soaring productivity.

Today, the study of a raft of economic activities finds incentive structures to be a centerpiece, and workplaces' acceptance of the concept of incenting staffers is fierce and well-developed. The vast majority of North American corporations and the managers that drive them believe in the redemptive power of rewards and feature at least a nod to their value in their strategies. Tying compensation in the form of a whole garden's worth of carrots to employees' achievements is common practice, and its effectiveness is well understood.

The science behind reward

Outside of psychology departments and parenting classes, people don't typically spend a lot of time thinking about the nuances of reward. Nor do they focus a lot on the distinction between intrinsic and extrinsic motivation. To assume they're interchangeable or that the two concepts can simply be added together for best effect is a mistake, point out those with expertise in this field. They're actually quite discernible from one another, and the key to understanding their most effective application is to appreciate that.

Here's the thing: in the theory of intrinsic reward, it's all about internal motivation. It's no secret that we experience a personal sense of pleasure for a job well done in the form of private pride or a sense of accomplishment. Adhere to a fitness schedule you've set for yourself or finish a book you've been meaning to read or refrain from eating Whoppers for a week, and feel good in your soul. That's intrinsic reward. Extrinsic rewards, however, are different. These are demonstrations of acknowledgment that are furnished by someone else. It is in this territory that employee incentive programs mostly reside.

The distinction is an important one. When behavior is intrinsically motivated, an individual's perceived locus of causality is thought to be internal; that is, individuals feel that task accomplishment is inside their own control. When people receive extrinsic rewards for a certain show of behavior, they will perceive their locus of causality to be external, and so will engage in it in anticipation of a forthcoming extrinsic reward.

And that's the case even if you're a dog.

It was more than a hundred years ago that Russian physiologist Ivan Pavlov threw back the covers on his twelve works of research and introduced the world to the theory of classical conditioning.

It was while he was studying digestion in his laboratory of pooches that Pavlov noticed a connection between his assistant's arrival in the room and his dogs' propensity to salivate. The promise of a reward had stimulated an active response, he noted. And it was thus that the Pavlovian effect, wherein a certain trigger reliably motivates a reaction in a sentient recipient, entered our general consciousness. It was an important discovery that had far-reaching applications. From potty training to presidential grooming, it was now widely understood that introducing certain prompts encourages very particular responses.

Can boss/leaders hire people they just like? Can boss/leaders hire people of a certain gender, for example? I like the introduction of blind hiring — for example, many orchestras went to blind auditions in the 1950s. This concept was done to assist in better selection. Actual screens are used to conceal the identity and gender of the musician from the jury, leading to newer levels of true objectivity in selections.

When new objectivity is introduced, we tend to get better decisions. For the music world, this concept of blind "interviews" created a new path to overcome gender-biased hiring: a vast majority of symphony orchestras revised their hiring practices. In the five highest-ranked orchestras in the US, the percentage of female musicians increased from 6 percent in 1970 to over 30 percent in 2018. It is refreshing to see the end result today, when I visit the Four Seasons opera house in Toronto. I think this group of wonderful musicians is now almost 50 percent female. With very few new orchestras starting, and low turnover found in most symphony orchestras, this was a very important development in hiring.

Findings on blind hiring

Quoted from "Orchestrating Impartiality: The Impact of 'Blind' Auditions on Female Musicians," by Claudia Goldin and Cecilia Rouse, *American Economic Review* 90:4 (2000):

> "Blind" auditions for symphony orchestras reduced sex-biased hiring and improved female musicians' likelihood of advancing out of preliminary rounds, which often leads to tenured employment.
>
> - Using a screen to conceal candidates from the jury during preliminary auditions increased the likelihood that a female musician would advance to the next round by eleven percentage points. During the final round, "blind" auditions increased the likelihood of female musicians being selected by 30 percent.
> - According to analysis using roster data, the transition to blind auditions from 1970 to the 1990s can explain 30 percent of the increase in the proportion female among new hires and possibly 25 percent of the increase in the percentage female in the orchestras.

- In short, "blind" auditions significantly reduced gender-biased hiring and the gender gap in symphony orchestra compositions.

In 2009, psychologists Mark R. Lepper and David Greene from Stanford and the University of Michigan were among a great clutch of academics that undertook studies designed to explore this concept further. They divided a group of preschoolers who loved to draw into three groups: those who were told they'd get a reward if they participated in a drawing test, those who were not told about the reward until after the exercise, and those who didn't receive a prize at all.

The study found that among children who expected a reward the spontaneous interest in drawing sank, while the other two groups of kids — the ones not expecting rewards — were more motivated to participate in the activity.

It was a lesson that legions of managers, industrial psychologists and Fortune 500 companies would take on board and mindfully apply to their own environments. Its transition to the corporate world was an easy one. Positively engaging employees and providing them with recognition and rewards improves performance. Full stop. Better yet, tie the reward in to the personality of each employee uniquely, and you can "double down" on success. I have seen sharp-as-a-tack sales leaders, trained in the use of the Predictive Index software, smartly tie sales contests in to the personalities of their sales and implementation teams. I call this giving employees a "second paycheck."

What does a reward/incentive program look like?

A comprehensive reward/incentive system needs to address four distinct areas of a worker's professional life: compensation, benefits, recognition and appreciation. Additionally, it should recognize and reward two types of employee activity: performance and behavior. Performance is the easiest to address because of the direct link between the initial goals a company sets for its employees and the final outcomes that result. The best example of this can be found in the way key salespeople typically get recognized for attaining certain goals.

The business of rewarding specific behaviors that have made a difference to your company is the more complicated sibling to simply rewarding performance. Here, a manager needs to consider the precise metrics of what she's compensating her employees for and what behaviors she's seeking to celebrate with any kind of reward. Less refined managers might get lost in the idea of compensating employees for time spent tapping a keyboard at their desk rather than pushing against the status quo limitations of their workplace with some kind of innovation. The difference between the two is significant.

Being part of a club

Everybody wants to be part of a club. Especially clubs that reward their high-performing members for jobs well done and that are considered desirable and elite. We all have a style in the way we like to get rewards. My father-in-law, Rod Stamler, was a brilliant award-winning assistant commissioner of the RCMP. He was head of commercial crime units and narcotics units for thirty-four years. When he retired, he should've been nominated for the Order of Canada. But he said, no, I don't want to go onstage. Put my team onstage.

All of the members of the band the Tragically Hip got the Order of Canada together. That was a great example of how to give recognition to a band — as a collective. You would never have done that individually. Alex Trebek was given it privately and individually. He seems to be a private guy. Donald Trump wants to be onstage all the time, to take credit for everything. Tying how you reward someone in to their personality is key.

Rewards vs. incentives

And while we're thinking about distinguishing between component parts of a concept, any consideration of the value of rewards and incentives in a professional environment needs to distinguish between the notion of a reward and the notion of an incentive. Because while employers use both human resource management techniques to manage and motivate their workforce, there are technical peculiarities that exist between the manner in which each mechanism is employed for this purpose.

Let's unpack these twin concepts.

A reward is a benefit that's given in recognition of an individual's particular acts of achievement, service, commendable behavior etc., after they have provided evidence of same. It exists to show employees that are performing well that their work and effort are valued and to motivate them to continue with them and, indeed, to improve the quality of their work. Importantly, a reward is offered only *after* a job is completed and the employee has demonstrated his worth.

An incentive, on the other hand, is a benefit that's promised to employees who are not performing to par. It is intended to motivate them to up their efforts and improve their overall behavior, productivity and output. As opposed to awaiting a final outcome that cries for acknowledgment, a manager introduces an incentive preemptively. The timing piece helps us understand that a reward, therefore, is more about celebrating a job well done, whereas an incentive is introduced as a means to bring about a behavior or action.

A more successful approach to driving your greatest impact from a rewards and recognition plan would be to map the rewards to the social style of the employee you want to celebrate.

Swiss psychologist Carl Jung was a pioneer of social styles. In the early twentieth century, he studied assertiveness and responsiveness. Jung created some of the world's best-known psychological concepts and developed analytics that could assist leaders with appreciating the essential complexity of extraversion and introversion.

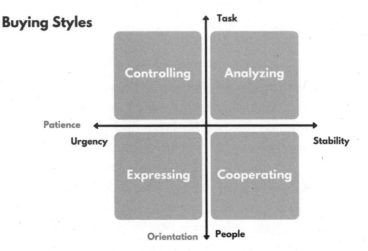

Buying Styles

Source: the Predictive Index®, a registered trademark of Predictive Index LLC and used here with permission.

For example, if you have a top sales leader who has the "expressing" social style, your reward plan will be dramatically different than for an employee who is an "analyzer." We are all selling our ideas to both employees and candidates and internal thought partners. There are predictable styles people bring with them to work and to play. These are observable behaviors that assist a boss in her communication events. For example, an expressing employee likes to be able to be in social situations as much as they can. This can be a blessing and a challenge for them. Many top salespeople are expressers. There could be a danger of expresser-to-expresser communication. Whose ego is larger here? Convincing the expresser is made easier with testimonials, since they like doing what the good leaders are doing out in the marketplace.

On the other hand, in the top right box of the four people styles we see the analyzer. This boss/leader or employee is a totally different cat. The analyzer will be direct and to the point: no pleasantries. The analyzer employee will be technical, logical. This style likes to talk about policies and procedures, planning and forecasting, systems and analysis and real solutions. Two very different worlds, in which the boss needs two very different approaches.

Rewards? What rewards?

As much as the innovation and excitement in the world of rewards and incentives swirls around booty quite outside the humdrum of cash, it must be acknowledged that humdrum cash has its virtues. It's a rare soul who's able to turn down a fistful of dollars for doing something successfully. So, in our inventory of the complement of rewards and incentives a mindful manager might consider, let's first explore the possibilities on the monetary side of the ledger.

Monetary rewards

When business owners think of reward systems, they typically put dosh at the top of the list. There's nothing wrong with that; nobody wants to work for free, which explains why the most popular incentives reward workers for their performance and productivity with money. This can take a range of forms: salary increments, bonuses, commissions, payments linked to the achievements of previously established targets, paid time off and straight-up cash awards.

Annual or semi-annual bonuses linked to job performance are also popular monetary incentives. Among other things, they're considered useful for the friendly competition they inspire among associates. Ideally, a winning rewards and incentive program should include some type of these longer-term rewards for key individuals. This has historically included some form of equity ownership or profit-sharing plans.

Non-monetary rewards

Management consultant W. Edwards Deming once famously declared, "Pay is not a motivator." While the notion seems superficially flawed considering the thirst most of us have for money and the things we want and need that it will buy, the statement has been proven to have merit. A parade of studies over the last few decades has found that when managers are asked to speculate on what matters most to their subordinates, they assume money tops the list. But when the question is put to them more explicitly — as in, "What do you care about?" — pay typically ranks only fifth or sixth.

A recent *Washington Post* article endorsed the same point of view when it argued that the "annual raise was turning into a relic of the pre-crisis economy as companies turn to creative — and cheaper — ways to compensate their employees." Increasingly, the piece noted, companies were recompensing their staffers with prizes that had nothing to do with currency.

And so an acknowledgment that monetary compensation is key to employee engagement is just one part of the rewards/incentive story. The other piece is a solid appreciation for the reality that rewards can exist in both monetary *and* non-monetary form. And a manager's ability to mindfully wrap their head around this can make all kinds of difference to a company's ability to attract and retain talent — to say nothing of its bottom line.

And there's no shortage of creative extrinsic rewards that reach beyond the limitations of cold, hard cash. Showing appreciation to your employees by acknowledging excellent performance and the kind of behavior you want to encourage is efficiently done through simple expressions and statements. Shoot an employee an email that congratulates them on an accomplishment or stop by his desk to convey your appreciation in person. Or you might alert a wider audience to your pleasure by issuing a public statement of thanks in front of an employee's co-workers or team, citing specific examples of what they did that positively impacted the organization.

Beyond that, the sky's the limit. Think schedule flexibility, training opportunities, the ability to work independently and extended health-care coverage. What about trips, tickets to events, audiences with celebrities and dinners out? And don't forget the enduring appeal of the ubiquitous but always appreciated gift card. The list is limited only by a manager's imagination. Indeed, the more creative the non-monetary perks and opportunities with which a company seeks to inspire its workers, the more appealing.

Finally, it's worth noting that great corporate cultures exist as their own form of reward. A working environment that offers its staffers a sense of purpose and acknowledgment is already rewarding their efforts in a genuinely meaningful way.

Employee recognition

Employee recognition is an incentive managers utilize to offer feedback and encouragement to their subordinates. It's a good thing. Employees who receive recognition for their work accomplishments tend to have increased morale and more positive attitudes about their workplaces. Along with regular bouts of verbal praise, employee recognition rewards might appear in the form of newsletter announcements, award ceremonies and Hall of Fame walls in office common spaces.

Gallup has found that employees who work in productive and engaged workplaces get some kind of recognition every seven days. Lots of that comes courtesy of peer-recognition programs that facilitate employees' acknowledgment of one another.

Aviva, one of the world's leading insurance companies, is often lauded for its evolved reward system, a highlight of which is the "peer recognition scheme." Here, staff can nominate individuals from among their 22,000 colleagues for bonuses by way of a sophisticated electronic system. Line managers consider nominees and award a particular number of points to deserving employees, who can then choose their own rewards.

Employee assistance programs

While every evolved workplace already has at least a basic employee assistance program in place, extras that extend its reach make for practical and attractive inclusions in an employer's toolbox. With an overarching objective to help workers maintain a balance between work and home life by supporting their mental and physical well-being, these inducements might include discount memberships at fitness centers and programs that help working parents find daycare and other activities for their children. Wellness programs that enhance the standard health-care offerings in an employment setting are also big on this front. Think here of things like massage, yoga, tai chi and Reiki.

Other non-monetary incentive suggestions

- Promotion (the assertive, proactive and tenacious [high A, low C Predictive Index] love this).

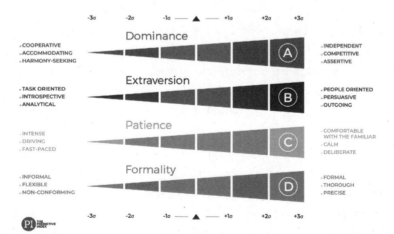

Source: the Predictive Index®, a registered trademark of Predictive Index LLC and used here with permission.

- An advancement of an employee's rank or position in an organizational hierarchy system (when mapped to personality, title changes can be really impactful).
- A pizza party (all of the team wins).
- Ferris Bueller's Day Off (an afternoon at a baseball game).
- The opportunity to swap offices with the boss for a week.
- A prime parking spot (the big-ego and high-persuasive love this one).
- A day off work (status win).
- The opportunity for the employee to ditch the project they like the least.
- A month-long public transit pass (functional).
- A continuing-education class (all high-sequence, high-detail employees love this).
- A new office chair (sends a message that you're part of a family and are cared about).
- Free home cleaning, like Shopify offers.

Any of these can be done with smaller companies. In fact, they are often easier in companies with fewer than fifty employees. It is also more important to bring in low-cost employee engagement ideas since it may be tougher to hire that great employee when your company brand is not well known. The modern working world is increasingly recognizing the value of incentives. By motivating workers effectively, leaders can steer people's choices in lucrative, abundant, useful directions.

The Incentive Federation, an American organization founded in 1984 as an alliance of associations involved in various aspects of the incentive field, describes the best incentive programs as those that "promote or encourage specific actions by a specific audience to produce measurable outcomes through integrated motivational strategies during a defined time period."

Do you have one in place? Does it check all those boxes? It's always a good time to review your strategic reward system and evaluate its effectiveness. Consider such questions as whether it's aligned with your other business strategies, whether it's driving the right behaviors for your company and whether it's advancing your overall performance goals. If it's lacking, mindfully address the ways in which it is. A solid, comprehensive, thoughtful rewards and incentives program can mean the difference between a business's success and its failure.

Chapter 8

The Mindfulness of Succession

"One of the things we often miss in succession planning
is that it should be gradual and thoughtful, with lots of
sharing of information and knowledge and perspective,
so that it's almost a non-event when it happens."

— ANNE M. MULCAHY

Managing and growing a business is no small feat. The exercise,
typically drawn out over many bootstrapped years, calls for a
massive store of patience, dedication, hard work, sacrifice and
money. But as much as creating a thriving new corporate entity
is taxing in the extreme, there's no shortage of entrepreneurs
who would sooner engage in it than have to embark on the
painstaking path of replacement planning (a much preferable
term to the standard "succession planning," for the wider berth
it gives to a company's natural HR movement).

It was 2012 when the Canadian Federation of Independent
Business declared that, while 54 percent of its members planned
to retire within five years, a mere 9 percent of them had written

up a formal plan to describe it. A survey performed the same year by the American Institute of Certified Professional Accountants found that 54 percent of multi-owner firms didn't have any written material to guide their succession efforts, and this in spite of the fact that 79 percent of business owners considered succession planning a significant issue in the next decade. And around the same time, KPMG, on behalf of the Canadian Association of Family Enterprise (CAFE), found that a mere 11 percent of the 322 family businesses it surveyed had succession plans for their CEOs. In its 2012 report, CAFE pointed to this lack of planning as a root cause of why only 30 percent of family businesses survive to the second generation (and only 15 percent reach the third).

Business owners put off this essential for a wide range of reasons. Some are daunted by the formidable nature of the task. Others don't appreciate how pressing it is and reject it for not being quicker or less involved. And for some folks, the notion of having to relinquish control to someone else is simply too unpalatable to really sink their teeth into. And so they don't.

But with more than 1.14 million small businesses in Canada and over eleven million in the US, and a serious chunk of their

Canadian Organizations Face Serious Leadership Succession Challanges

The Conference Board of Canada
Insights You Can Count On

- **Ottawa, April 16, 2014 - As many senior and second-level executives retire or approach retirement, Canadian organizations face serious succession challenges.**
- **For every two senior executives, organizations have only one job-ready, or near job-ready successor.**

owners within two-decade earshot of the retirement bell, replacement planning is more important than ever. And it's not enough to simply add the task to your to-do list and strike it after a perfunctory run at it. Pulling the succession-planning trick off mindfully takes a special kind of focus. What could be more critical, after all, than to be present in the all-encompassing task of choosing a plan for how a company will evolve into its next incarnation?

Replacement planning: unpacking the term

A succession plan is a formal document that outlines a blueprint for how a company is going to transition from one state to another. Most typically, it refers to the transfer of ownership and leadership from one individual to another, often because of retirement, though it could also be associated with a switch in management structure or the sale of the firm. An exit strategy may also become necessary if an owner feels declining passion for the business. For many entrepreneurial owners, once the excitement of getting a business off the ground fades, the pleasure of engagement fades. There is a problem in Canada where we see a lack of "backfill" of potential leaders.

The World Economic Forum on the global outlook for 2015 called lack of leadership the number-three challenge facing the global economy. Eighty-six percent of the Survey on the Global Agenda's 1,767 respondents said there is a leadership crisis. Also in 2015, the Center for Creative Leadership surveyed 2,239 leaders from twenty-four organizations in three countries and found existing crucial leadership skills weren't enough to meet current and future needs.

Whatever the impetus that inspires it, replacement planning is the process of identifying and developing employees to fill key positions in an organization when human resources leave it empty. When this is undertaken mindfully, it adequately prepares the business to carry on without a hitch after individuals retire or leave the operation for other reasons — some of which, like death or disability, can be thrust upon the company suddenly. It ensures that key positions are consistently staffed with precisely the talent they call for. It can also prepare an organization for expansion or reorganization.

Broadly speaking, replacement planning is about developing employees and supporting them in their careers to ensure that an organization is reliably equipped not only with the expertise but the temperaments to keep it humming without a glitch. By casting a mindful eye to the subject on a regular basis, a manager ensures that the exodus of key workers takes place smoothly, and never lets the organization become deprived of the knowledge and skill sets it needs.

Failing to plan for business succession can create a bad scene for a company, which can pay the price of significant revenue loss for its unpreparedness. The business itself could even get lost in a ham-fisted shuffle. A staggering number of small businesses and partnerships without solid succession plans fail when the owner or a senior-level partner retires, becomes incapacitated or dies. What's more, the partners left to pick up the pieces from such calamities can introduce new complications to an already floundering situation if they're unable to agree on next steps. There's nothing like strife among partners to close a company down.

Finally, to be truly effective, a succession plan must include a regular review by the board in an exercise that takes into consideration both the current staff complement and any relevant industry and market developments. (Succession considerations aside, an annual review by a company's board is always valuable for the temperature it takes of the talent in the company.)

Why replacement planning's important

Providing key leadership through critical strategic projects is important to both the short- and long-term success of a company in its ongoing bid to achieve the objectives of ownership. But you already know that. You're a business owner, after all, and have seen your company through all manner of evolutionary blips. This next one — succession and all of its attendant details — is a biggie.

Some changes just flop. One of the best-planned succession failures was in the marketing for the transition to "New Coke" in 1985. The Coke team of researchers only focused on the physical packaging. What they failed to grasp was that while subjects could appreciate changed physical characteristics like taste and branding, Coca-Cola also had symbolic significance to buyers, particularly in the American market. For a group that prefers tradition over novelty, New Coke couldn't hold a candle to the continuity and familiarity of Old Coke (or, as it was eventually rebranded, Coca-Cola Classic). I liken this to a company culture, an employee brand. Too radical a change could spell disaster.

Market research isn't just a numbers game. In failing to capture feeling and attitude toward the brand and relying on taste tests alone, Coca-Cola was left with a ton of product, cranky consumers and a big corporate black eye. People change is also not just a numbers game. All successful people changes are part science, part golden gut. We also always need to add in the boss. To forget to factor in who the people will be working for would be like doing a "Old Coke to New Coke" change: risky.

Think of your employees as beakers of knowledge, each of them a vessel for a discrete cache of specialized skills, training and information. As they stroll about the offices, drifting from boardroom to breakroom, they carry with them all of this usefulness. Indeed, the contract they have with their employers allows the company access to these intangibles at its pleasure. But when an employee exits a business, they take that unique stash of particular expertise and experience with them. That's significant. Employers that are unprepared to cope with the knowledge gaps these departures present can be left scrambling to run their day-to-day operations.

Beyond that, there's no question that replacement planning has a bearing on the market valuations of companies. It does, too, on the confidence business associates have in companies and in the morale of their employees. Smart approaches here also help retain valuable workers and lower the costs of recruiting new talent — major considerations as the world's workforces age. And for the individual employees in question, the exercise can also prove enriching for the help it offers them in realizing career plans and aspirations.

Any discussion in which company principals can engage around succession is worthwhile. Indeed, boards often emerge from these conversations with a clearer sense of their mission and business goals. And their reach beyond the succession focus can reveal other opportunities for corporate improvement. It's not uncommon for a board to overhaul its entire business model in a sweep that extends well beyond the succession realm in these scenes.

Finally, replacement planning is important because it safe-guards a company's accumulated stores of trust, respect and goodwill for transfer to the new guard of corporate leaders. Deliberate and systematic plans by organizations to ensure they "live" include

- a leadership continuity plan for key positions;
- a process to develop intellectual and knowledge capital for the future;
- encouragement of individual advancement.

Replacement planning: timing

Hard-and-fast rules around the timing of replacement planning are in short supply, but a solid rule of thumb has a forward-looking business owner tackling the question some five years out from the anticipated date of exodus. The business transfer date could be a milestone, such as the owner's sixty-fifth birthday or his fortieth year at the helm of the business. The important thing in setting the business transition date is to ensure it allows a period of years rather than months for the business transfer to ultimately take place. This way, there's enough of a built-in cushion to be thoughtful about this critical matter.

Succession planning systems have traditionally been shrouded in secrecy to avoid draining motivation from those not on the fast track. The idea was that if you don't know where you stand (and you stand on a bottom rung), you will continue to strive to climb the ladder.

Today's employees are asking for clarity. It is a new world; to achieve transparency, companies and organizations need simple systems that are easy to use, with immediate but secure access for participants.

Software and mapping technology — and, in particular the internet — are powerful enablers. Workforce Analytics tools like Predictive Index give data on gaps between potential and present roles.

The danger, of course, is of assigning yourself a deadline so far in the future that it risks getting lost in the pressing concerns of the present. The demands of running a business are constant (no kidding), and while most firms appreciate the importance of planning for an evolving HR reality, the actual application of same sometimes loses out to more immediate concerns. Take care not to let that happen.

Mapping it out

So many times in succession planning, it's shirtsleeves to shirt-sleeves in three generations. What happens is the second and third generations become so spoiled that they don't have the same drive and behavior as the first. Everything's been given to them. That's a problem.

Analytics can come in and say, What does my organization look like? We do maps. If I have a detail-oriented builder and project manager, and then I've got someone here who's never said no to me, who always did what I told her to do, and I'm leaving and she has to set direction and the independent agenda, she'll struggle because she's never been asked to do that. Put her in that role, and it'll spin out of control.

There's a great story at the Greater Toronto Airports Authority, where I was brought in to do a team-building event. The GTAA operates Pearson, one of the largest airports in North America. There was an engineer there who was technical, harmonious, sequential, methodical and extremely detailed. After about fourteen years, he'd done his time, and it was his turn to be moved into a project manager role — much more independent, more directional, more take-charge, which is the total opposite of his harmonious approach. Much more persuasive, dealing with variety, multitasking, working simultaneously on multiple files. He was thrust into the role and hated it. Every day he had to turn himself inside out. He was the wrong successor and ended up having to go on stress leave. It was a sad story. He said, if only we'd had analytics.

When it comes to the succession of her business, every business owner is ultimately faced with choosing between two options: it will be an event planned and controlled by her, or it will be an unplanned occurrence brought on by outside forces. That the first scenario typically results in a happier scene, both financially and emotionally, should surprise no one.

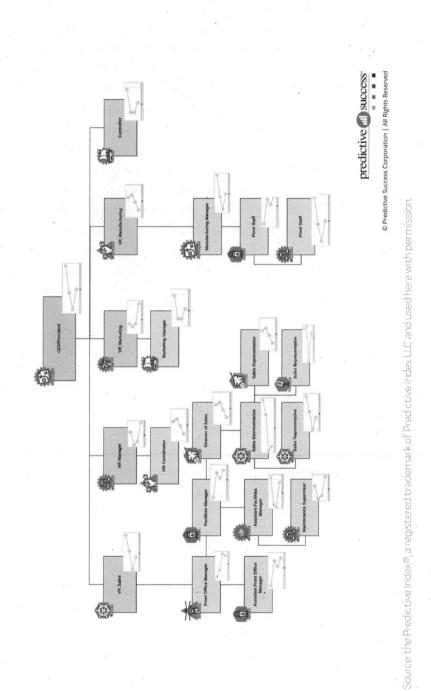

So let's focus on that one.

Business leaders should prepare for replacement planning and talent development as they would any critical processes in the enterprise. That means, first, determining the challenges, industry trends and development needs their organization will face in the next five to seven years. With those in hand, next up comes a development of a list of the competencies and characteristics they require of a successor. From there, it's a cakewalk: identify a pool of candidates whose bona fides align with the list, and name a successor.

While there's no standard template to guide a company's journey from one set of hands to the next, there are various components that should be included in a succession plan. For one, every successful succession plan begins with determining the objectives of the owners. For another, it needs to take into account the business's existing organizational and management structure.

And it should include a nod to the company's future growth trajectory.

Every outgoing owner has been the leader of the business for some time. They have usually developed personal relationships with key personnel. These relationships need to be taken into account in a conversation about business succession.

It's also important to consider a business's philosophy and culture in replacement planning. A company that feels strongly about a set of fundamental core values can use them to inform a mindful planning process that guides all its decisions related to replacing key personnel.

Another important phase of the planning process looks at conducting a business valuation of the business entity. This piece, critical to establishing the financial portion of the plan, requires the participation of an experienced valuation analyst. Once the value of the business has been determined, the structure of the transaction in terms of income, gift and estate tax can be tackled, along with financing.

A plan that pays heed to all of these essentials will confer critical stability and continuity on the company.

Breaking up the task

One way to ensure that a succession plan mindfully manages the transition from one set of leaders/owners to the next is to undertake it strategically. That means making sure there's lots of time for it to get shuffled up and down a company's to-do list, and tackling its bulk by dividing the big picture into a bunch of smaller ones. By divvying up your overarching target into achievable goalposts along the way, you increase the likelihood of meeting them.

Get started by holding a replacement planning day with all the key stakeholders from your firm. Declare the event a brainstorming session, where no idea's off limits. Refine and focus your conversation as you go.

After they've developed a rough template for the component pieces of the exercise, business owners should ask themselves a number of questions:

- How will I exit the business?
- Do I want to sell my business or develop a plan whereby I can transfer it to family or key management members?
- Is my business a candidate to go public?
- When do I want to take my leave of the company? (Or, at least, when do I believe I will slow down and commit less time to the firm?)
- Have I identified who will lead the firm in the future? (If it's children, are they willing and ready? If I'm selling to a third party, what shape must the business be in to attract the best price?)
- How committed is this person to the business?

- Do they have the management skills and business experience required to run the business?
- Will they be able to do more than just administer the business; can they develop and grow it?
- What do I need to do to ensure this new leader is ready to take the helm?
- What needs to take place between now and then in order that the business not be disrupted; that key employees, partners and clients are not put under undue stress; and that I maintain my standard of living?
- How do I exit the business in a manner that maximizes my financial gain without stinging me with a huge tax bill?
- Does my successor need any special training before they can take over?
- How will this transfer of ownership take place? Will it be in the form of a gift, a sale at fair market value, an estate freeze or something else altogether?

Figuring all of these details out calls for everyone at the table. Clear and honest communication among all your business's stakeholders and advisors is crucial.

The family piece

When an owner begins to think about retiring or cutting short the management of the business for some other reason, it makes sense that their first choice would be to look at family members as replacements. After all, you know these folks. You've known them for years. You've watched them grow. And you see them all the time at Thanksgiving, anyway. Easy-peasy, right?

Not necessarily.

The transfer of a business from one family member to another can be fraught. Sharing a bloodline, as it turns out, is no guarantee of a seamless and pain-free transition. Indeed, it could be argued that a business successor who hails from the same gene pool brings a whole additional slew of challenges compared to the non-related alternative. Interpersonal relationships can quickly complicate and even sink a business transaction.

No wonder more than half of all businesses transferred to the second generation fail in the first three years (and that less than 20 percent of those second-generation successors will successfully transition the business to the third generation). With this population of business owners, then, a commitment to mindful replacement planning is more important than ever.

But the familial connections notwithstanding, there's no question that this is first, last and always a business transaction. So minimize the potential for conflict and financial loss by developing a plan that addresses all of the possible issues — around legalities, taxation, valuation, company vision, etc. — that could crop up. And don't forget the impact of business-ownership transfer on non-family members actively involved in the management of the business.

Selling your business

There are many ways to sell a business, but not all of them include the unloading of the full corporate entity as a going concern. As much as selling might make the most apparent sense, some businesses simply don't lend themselves to a profitable big-picture sale that will support a retirement plan. If yours is one of these exceptions, you might consider selling its shares rather than its assets. Or maybe you transfer the operating business to a holding company and then sell the assets or shares of that. There are different tax implications with each of these routes.

In some cases, the business assets may fetch a better price and be easier to sell without any liabilities. In others, an owner might consider selling the following elements of their business:

- its intellectual property;
- its customer base;
- its established distribution channels.

The nine-box grid

Predictive analytics like the Predictive Index ramp up the objectivity in planning for succession changes with fairness and data. Consider, by way of illustration, the nine-box grid (see graphic). The nine-box grid is an individual assessment tool that evaluates both an employee's current contribution to the organization and his or her potential level of contribution to the organization. The nine-box grid is a simple table graph that rates "potential" on the y, or vertical, axis and "performance" on the x, or horizontal, axis. In other words, the vertical columns of the grid identify an individual employee's growth potential within the organization, and the horizontal rows identify whether the employee is below, meeting or exceeding performance expectations in their current role.

The nine-box grid is most commonly used in replacement planning as a method of evaluating an organization's talent pool and identifying potential leaders. When used in this arena, the x-axis assesses leadership performance and the y-axis assesses leadership potential. The combination of the x- and y-axes determines where the leader is placed in the nine-box grid. Individuals in the upper right quadrant (Box 1) will then be identified as high-potential candidates in the company's succession plan.

For performance appraisal purposes, the nine-box grid provides a simple visual reference that can include appraisal and assessment data to allow managers to easily view employees' actual and potential performance. Individual developmental plans for both high- and low-performing employees can then be designed with collaboration from the employees' managers and the HR department.

A sample nine-box grid might look something like this:

x-axis (Performance) >>> y-axis (Potential) ↑↑↑	Underperformance, not "cutting it." Probably in the role job model for them. Or with the wrong manager. Could become a "silent killer" if we do not deal with them.	Effective Performance. They grind it out, are engaged and effective.	Outstanding Performance, totally there, cultural champion
High Potential	**Box 5** Seasoned professional capable (does not mean job ready now) of expanded role, but may be experiencing problems that require coaching and mentoring.	**Box 2** Does extremely well at current job with potential to do more; give stretch assignments to help prepare for next level. With a high cognitive score we can drive more work, more assignments perhaps.	**Box 1** Consistently performs well in a variety of assignments; superstar employee. Big-picture thinker, problem-solver, self-motivated. Just there; we cannot lose this person.
Medium Potential	**Box 8** With coaching, could progress within level; focus on stretch goals for this employee. If we lose this employee it will not damage our business unit.	**Box 6** May be considered for job enlargement at the same level, but may need coaching in several areas, including people management.	**Box 3** Still have work to do. Current role may still provide opportunity for growth/development; focused on tactical; focus should be on helping improve strategic thinking.
Low Potential	**Box 9** Consider moving them. A reclassification to a lower level or exit from the organization. Promote to "happy alumni" or out the door to "customer."	**Box 7** Effective performer, but may have reached career potential; try to coach employee or becoming more innovative, focus on lateral thinking.	**Box 4** A keeper. Still some leg room left. Experienced high performer but has reached limit of career potential. Still a valuable employee and can be encouraged to develop communication and delegation skills.

In coaching and talent management, the value of the nine-box grid is to identify when coaching or a change in job or responsibilities may be needed. It may not be valuable to the organization to spend time and effort attempting to salvage an individual with low potential and poor performance. However, an individual with low potential but effective performance may need to be engaged or motivated in his or her current job.

When used correctly, the nine-box grid can be a versatile and valuable tool for an organization — but HR professionals are advised to become thoroughly familiar with the concept before attempting to use it. Like any tool, it can be damaging to the organization if used incorrectly.

The 9 Box Talent Model

Enigma	**Growth Employee**	**Future Leader**
Dilemma	**Core Employee**	**High Impact Performer**
Under Performer	**Effective**	**Trusted Professional**

Potential ↑ · Performance →

After GE/McKinsey

Source: www.predictivesuccess.com/blog/9-box/

Staying on top

Replacement planning is an ongoing process. By constantly evaluating and making revisions to it as you approach its deadline, you can keep adapting it to changing needs and circumstances. Ultimately, whether your organization's efforts on this front deliver a return on investment will depend on the original goals and how well identified they were. But it'll be a factor, too, of how sensitive a plan is to the evolving environment in which it exists. Consider how a constantly updating marketplace, personnel complement and technological scene can have an effect on a dynamic succession plan.

Test the continued relevance of yours by subjecting it to a few questions:

- Are the goals of the succession plan still appropriate?
- Has critical technology changed?
- Are there key positions that need to be added to the plan?
- Do any marketplace or government changes affect the plans for employee succession?

Above all, a review of a replacement plan is intended to ensure that the plan is doing what it was designed to do. The great volume of detail and attention you invested in the early part of the planning process may convince you that all the heavy lifting is done. It isn't. A successful replacement plan is so because of an ongoing campaign of oversight.

Exiting a business does not have to be a trying or negative experience. It can simply be a part of progressing toward an eventual goal, or a way of taking advantage of new opportunities. Being prepared for the next stage of your company's evolution with a sound, well-thought-out exit strategy means you can enjoy the pleasure of business ownership, secure in the knowledge that, when you take your leave of the place, you'll do so mindfully.

Chapter 9

The Mindful Use of Social Media

"Social media is an amazing tool, but it's really the face-to-face interaction that makes a long-term impact."
— FELICIA DAY

Social media has transformed the way humans communicate. Thanks to its ubiquitous presence, conversations are snappier than ever — and they're accompanied by the enriching offerings of videos and emojis and links for further intel.

Social media has altered great swaths of the modern economy. It's elemental in law enforcement, political protest organization, disaster preparedness, security at major events, emergency response and military intelligence. And in the business world, social media has rewritten marketing and advertising. Recruitment and retention. Branding and sales. Thanks to its pervasive presence, this game-changer offers companies an unprecedented opportunity to reach and cultivate audiences into which they can tap directly and on demand.

Suddenly, a revolution to the landscape means everyone's consumed with one question: how should organizations think about communicating with the public now that the public can communicate back?

Still, this relative newcomer to our daily world is a source of frustration as much as celebration. The content that tears across its bandwidth is open to wild misinterpretation, and the trouble that has erupted as a result of that over the years is legion. It exposes its sources to character attacks whose magnitude couldn't have been imagined before. And it offers a mouthpiece to reckless talkers whose pronouncements are often delivered without consideration for their reverberations.

Mindfulness, as it turns out, is as critical to social media as social media is to it. Let's dig in on how to marry the two.

What is social media?

Social media, it might be argued, is the best thing to happen to business since the Dictaphone. Here is an essentially free tool that almost everyone is using (either benefit or curse, depending on your approach), and which connects the world in a tremendous and extraordinary network. With it, businesses of all sizes can now create major marketing campaigns on shoestring budgets. It is a boon of unprecedented dimensions.

Generally speaking, when people talk about social media they're talking about the myriad web-based applications and interactive programs out there that facilitate the creation, discussion and exchange of user-generated content. The principal social media channels are Facebook, LinkedIn, YouTube, Twitter, Flickr, Instagram and Pinterest. Along with these, the medium includes blogs and microblogs, business networks, collaborative projects, enterprise social networks, forums, photo-sharing, product/service reviews, social bookmarking, social gaming, video-sharing and virtual worlds.

Mind you, not all social media platforms are relevant for business. Photo-sharing, social bookmarking and social gaming, for example, might not warrant the same interest from companies as platforms like YouTube, LinkedIn and Facebook. Product-reviewing websites, blogs, forums and social networks where customers share their experiences and data points are great vehicles for company enlightenment. And they're also excellent resources for recruitment and business networking.

The mindful piece

Mindfulness is about focusing on the present. When you're mindful, you're fully engaged in what's going on in the now. There's no room for distractions or diversions in a mindful state. Ironically, social media exists on quite the polar opposite of that plane. Indeed, in its essence, social media is all about distraction, about presenting an alternative that's attractive enough to pull a person's attention to it. A thousand articles and blogs have been penned on how to resist the lure of electronic communication. (No one mentions that the blogs themselves are the biggest culprits of all.)

Whatever one's position, the stuff is here to stay. And thank goodness for it. Social media means an entirely new opportunity for companies and marketers. And the challenge to distract visitors with content that engages them enough to yank their attention from all the rest. Better to regard it that way than as a source of worrisome distraction for your staffers.

Indeed, consider the concern that your employees might lose focus if they spend too much time on social media sites in this light: there's not much to balance anymore. Talking to people — over social media or otherwise — is a company's *real* job. By some accounts, 90 percent of a business's employee time is spent communicating with customers. And so, while employees have to continue to execute on the core competencies of the business, it's important to recast social media from a distraction to a necessity.

Best boss/leaders and social media

The corporate world was not a fast friend to social media in its earliest days. Indeed, lots of professional organizations struggled mightily to understand the communication powers that had been dropped in their laps, and they both under- and overplayed their early hands. It took a long, long time for the business world to appreciate the subtlety of the medium, and its early forays along social media thoroughfares were nothing short of stumbling displays of misuse.

And no wonder. We were an unaccustomed lot. In the days before Facebook's February 2004 appearance in our midst, the world was a smaller place. Back before Mark Zuckerburg had unveiled a social tool designed to expose members of the population to one another in a medium that had no precedent (in North America, at least), no one had any concept of the enormous capacity for sharing with which we were about to be blessed. In that pre-revolutionary stretch, companies communicated with the outside world through much more traditional means: direct mail, cold calls, conventional advertising, old-fashioned written correspondence — and not much else. This tight collection of communication avenues meant a brand's dimensions were much easier to contain and control.

Today, all bets are off. Social media means a multiplication of means to communicate. But it also renders all of the world's companies public entities, vulnerable to the scrutiny and criticism of everyone around them. This vast new dimension has exploded the exposure of organizations that used to be able to control their message. That's a daunting development, and one that threw people for a serious loop in the early days. Still, lots of time has passed since then, and the corporate world has now wrapped its collective brain around the rules for playing this game. The value of participating in social media is well understood now, and sophistication in how to most profitably conduct oneself in this field is finely developed.

Take social media's power to influence buying decisions, for one. Today, businesses are well versed on that aspect of this social force, and are exploiting it with both abandon and impressive precision. In a landmark study by McKinsey in mid-2015, the global management consulting firm discovered that social recommendations are at the root of more than a quarter of all purchases made. That figure, extracted from a survey of some 20,000 European consumers, was a surprise. Statisticians had previously estimated that just between 10 and 15 percent of purchases are influenced by recommendations that shoot across fiber-optic cables.

And the communication flows in the other direction too. It's social media, after all, that has expanded the general public's ability to connect with companies that would otherwise have been arm's-length outliers reachable only through concerted effort. With social media, customers can approach consumer goods organizations with questions and complaints. And using social customer service in return, the companies in their receipt can sidestep costly labor-intensive telephone calls. Bots can point inquirers to the appropriate areas of their website or to livechat, and the entire transaction can take place, in theory, without any corporate fingers being lifted. The British communications giant BT has employed social media customer service to deflect 600,000 contacts a year from the phones. That translates into £2-million annual savings (2014 figures).

In 2010, we saw a great example of what communication flow being stopped cold can do to an industry. The airspace closures in Europe resulting from the eruption of the Eyjafjallajökull volcano on April 14 led to the disruption of some 100,000 flights and ten million passenger journeys. KLM Airlines, whose social customer care famously came into its own when many flights were grounded in the wake of the Icelandic ash cloud, is renowned in its industry and beyond for being ahead of the curve in response time. Here was great insight from a team of prepared boss/leaders.

Extensive research from Investis on how large companies in the UK and US are using social media for corporate communications offers some useful revelations into how social media can benefit companies. It shows that there's been a rise in the FTSE 100 companies linking their corporate websites to social media, from 35 percent three years ago to 72 percent today, and a rise of US S&P 100–linked companies from 61 percent to 89 percent. And the tactic's working:

- Companies engaging with social media are gaining more views and social interaction.
- On Facebook alone, companies who respond to wall posts get more likes than those who do not acknowledge.
- Companies tweeting thirty times or more each month averaged 20,800 followers, compared to 2,456 from those who were tweeting less.

There are legion ways in which a company's engagement along social media channels enhances its existence. Consider the following:

- **Brand awareness. Your people also are your brand.** Regardless of where a prospect is on their buying cycle, your appearance in their feed has the power to jolt them into cognizance mode in a way that might not have been possible before. I see the personality of the CEO to set the tone for the people brand in most companies.
- **Cultivation of trust, the journey to creating more trust deposits.** A company that has lots of followers or streams of positive commentary on its pages gets

an automatic buy-in. Everybody wants to be part of something that's well loved and popular, after all.

- **A direct route to influencers.** Social media identifies the pathways to corporate decision-makers like nothing else. This powerful tool serves as an amazing introduction maker that facilitates relationships and engenders trust — important for everyone hoping to capitalize on leads and sales. Social media "influencers" can be powerful, for better or worse, as was the case with the infamous 2017 Fyre Festival, which featured models Kendall Jenner, Bella Hadid, Emily Ratajkowski and others in social media campaigns promoting it as an upscale event on a private Bahamian island. In reality, the festival failed to provide attendees with more than basic necessities, and its founder was sentenced to prison on federal fraud charges. In 2019, a U.S. federal judge ruled that Jenner's company and agencies representing Hadid and Ratajkowski could be subpoenaed in the case.

- **Engagement with customers.** In 2015, Taco Bell lobbied for the creation of a taco emoji, and won. When users employed it in a tweet, they were rewarded with a custom piece of video content from the company. It was an amazing illustration of customer engagement in action. The publisher of the Predictive Index introduced personality "emojis" and Gen Z and millennials have loved them. Each to use and understand.

- **Sales conversion.** Similarly, your bursts of social media outreach serve as engagement opportunities like never before. The more points of connection with a potential client a company has, the more opportunity there is to convert one of them into a sale.

- **Shareable content.** Everyone knows that cute cat videos rule the web. If you've got one, or anything else that's darling or enlightening or amazing, you should share it and win points for the effort. It's a trick NASA knows all about. Its regular dissemination of astounding imagery and inspiring stories (alongside peer-reviewed science) explains its twenty-seven million Twitter followers. GE's great at this too. It recently teamed up with filmmaker Sam Cossman to document the company's installation of tracking sensors in the Masaya Volcano in Nicaragua. Cossman shared the dramatic results on Snapchat, Instagram and Facebook.

- **Insight into market trends.** Understanding what sorts of posts create the most engagement may help you to identify the kinds of problems your customers have.
- **The opportunity to celebrate yourself.** There's no shortage of opportunities on social media for companies to pat themselves on the back in full public view of the world. When outsiders see employees cheering about the fantastic scene at their company, credibility gets enhanced. L'Oréal encourages its staff to populate social media with posts about working there, using the hashtag #lifeatloreal.
- **Employee recruitment and retention.** Social media facilitates unprecedented organizational transparency. When would-be staffers look up your company, they can now find all the cards on the table. And for folks already on the payroll, there's nothing like a positive buzz about a place to make a person want to stay put.
- **Fresh opportunities for branding.** Social media has expanded a company's points of contact with its customers exponentially. Now, along with a website and a bunch of social media pages and tweets, an organization can even create its own channel and cultivate amazing connections over time. Coke TV is one illustration of how an organization's understanding of online video and influencers can produce a connection that's hard to put a value on.

Reputation: risk versus reward

In a recent wide-ranging study, Deloitte declared reputation the number-one strategic risk executives at large companies undertake. More than that, it found that social media is the biggest threat to their business models. The intersection between the two cannot be overlooked. There's no question that the digital presence a company puts forward for public consumption is vulnerable to meaningful judgment. Sometimes, the exposure proves too much to bear.

Take the ubiquitous product-review websites. What's written on places like Yelp, TripAdvisor and Angie's List can have a profound effect on a company's fortunes. But this content is typically outside of their control, which makes everything that happens there a bit of a crapshoot. That's where the risk comes in.

The best tool in the safeguarding of a company's reputation is a good social media policy. In this document should rest all of an organization's standards and expectations around its employees' social media usage. It should also explain what actions need to be taken in the event a mistake is made or a company social handle comes under attack (by trolls or hackers).

The importance of a social media policy

Essential to mastering social media is developing a strategy that makes plain a company's stance on all manner of social media quandaries. Social media policies outline corporate expectations around employees' social media use. They confront the question of how to maintain a corporate appearance of objectivity while allowing the individuals of a firm empowered expression. They preserve a brand's reputation while encouraging employees to responsibly share the company's message. They establish parameters around brand voice and tone, empower staffers to share company messaging and safeguard an organization against legal troubles and security risks by naming — and discussing how to avoid — them. They should also explain positions around use of images and how an employee should respond if they somehow put the company's reputation at risk.

No matter the size or age or preoccupation of your company, it needs a social media policy.

And there are other questions besides. What should an organization say on social media? Who should say it? Should CEOs tweet? What about corporate boards? Can employees comment in chat rooms? How should a company's social media presence tie in with the rest of its communications and marketing efforts? How should an organization respond to commenters? What if the commenters are being critical?

It's wise to get these questions addressed early and to boil the results into a digestible document that everyone who has anything to do with social media at the company can commit to memory. Organizations without benefit of hard and fast social media policies can easily flounder.

Take the conundrum that CNN's senior editor of Middle Eastern affairs, Octavia Nasr, found herself in after sending a tweet expressing respect for the Shia cleric Grand Ayatollah Mohammad Hussein Fadlallah. The news organization has pretty clear guidelines about how its employees need to represent it on the social media airwaves, and Nasr was dismissed without hesitation. Among its highlights is the point that CNN employees are "to avoid taking public positions on the issues and people and organizations on which we report." And they go on: "keep in mind that you should not be commenting or writing about what goes on in the workplace at CNN without specific approval by CNN senior managers."

We could also add in the daily use of Twitter by President Donald Trump as his force du jour.

Intel, meanwhile, includes these recommendations in its employee-facing social media oversight:

- Stick to your area of expertise and provide unique, individual perspectives on what's going on at Intel and in the world.
- Post meaningful, respectful comments — in other words, no spam and no remarks that are off-topic or offensive.
- Always pause and think before posting. That said, reply to comments in a timely manner, when a response is appropriate.
- Respect proprietary information and content, and confidentiality.
- When disagreeing with others' opinions, keep it appropriate and polite.
- Know and follow the Intel Code of Conduct and the Intel Privacy Policy.

Best Buy's social media policy includes a collection of emphatic "don't shares." To wit:

- *The numbers*: Non-public financial or operational information. This includes strategies, forecasts and most anything with a dollar-figure attached to it. If it's not already public information, it's not your job to make it so.
- *Promotions*: Internal communication regarding drive times, promotional activities or inventory allocations, including advance ads, drive time playbooks, holiday strategies and *Retail Insider* editions.
- *Personal information*: Never share personal information regarding other employees or customers.
- *Legal information*: Anything to do with a legal issue, legal case or attorneys.
- *Anything that belongs to someone else*: Let them post their own stuff; you stick to posting your own creations.

This includes illegal music sharing, copyrighted publications and all logos or other images that are trademarked by Best Buy.

- *Confidential information*: Do not publish, post or release information that is considered confidential or top secret.

Ford's social media policy has more of a holistic bent to it:

- Be honest about who you are.
- Make it clear that the views expressed are yours.
- You speak for yourself, but your actions represent those of Ford Motor Company.
- Use your common sense.
- Play nice.
- The internet is a public space.
- The internet remembers.
- An official response may be needed.
- Respect the privacy of offline conversations.
- Same rules and laws apply: new medium, no surprise.
- When in doubt, ask.

The takeaway? The modern company needs to craft a set of social media guidelines for itself. They need to be thorough and personal, particular and easy to follow. Badmouthing the competition is something to watch out for, though it's OK to point out your competitive advantages. Profanity's not cool; neither are insults about co-workers, supervisors or the workplace.

Filling the space

Once a company is convinced of social media's usefulness, the next step is understanding how to build an effective presence in the online world and how to create an ongoing ribbon of engaging content to populate it. This task might loom large for old-school marketers who've long understood word of mouth and straight-up advertising to be the most effective tactics for sharing the news about their organizations. These are the same people who might struggle with this new imperative to communicate their "story" effectively and who will endure a learning curve, no doubt, as they come to appreciate the full arsenal at their disposal in this brave new world.

Establishing an infrastructure to guide its content is one thing; determining the content itself is something else altogether. After all, you've got some pretty fair competition. Every sixty seconds in 2016, the following took place on the internet:

- 3.3 million Facebook posts were created;
- 3.8 million Google searches were performed;
- 65,972 Instagram photos were uploaded;
- 448,800 tweets were created;
- 1,440 WordPress posts were published;
- twenty-nine million WhatsApp messages were sent;
- 500 hours of video were uploaded;
- 149,513 emails were sent.

Taken as a digital whole, that's an awful lot of content. Wonder how to make yours stand out above the rest?

Here are four best practices to leverage in your pursuit of developing successful social channels and engaging your audience.

- **Pick platforms strategically.** A company's early, tentative steps into a social media marketing campaign can be taken more confidently if they involve tools that don't utterly intimidate. That means picking a single platform, to start, and committing unreservedly to understanding what it might do. It includes training a laser focus on updates and on finding and creating quality social content for just a single stage. You can branch out into additional platforms as you become comfortable and efficient with the first. It pays to start small and work up gradually.

- **Craft your profile cleverly.** Be sure to make the most of the opportunity your profile description affords to highlight important features and business information. And make sure your contact information's plain and prominent. Talk about the industries you serve, the services you offer, the capabilities you excel at. Include customer testimonials, if you have them. And photos, to break up dense text. If you're still at a loss, ask customers what they love about you. And don't get overwhelmed by the call for description — it's completely acceptable to just use short phrases or keywords.

- **Be consistent.** Once you've rolled yourself into multiple social media platforms, you've put the onus for consistency on yourself. That means maintaining a constant message and look across all of your social media appearances — logos, icons, points of view, key points. Regard this obligation as a bonus: it means duplicating your design across your spectrum, instead of having to be original in each instance. The uniformity gives your stuff a professional sheen too.

- **Publish according to schedule.** By establishing a timetable for attending to its social media accounts, a company compels itself to maintain its digital presence. Where possible, social media managers should assign content or at least topic areas to their anticipated tweets and posts. Consider linking days of the week with specific types of content (promotional on Monday, service on Tuesday, editorial on Wednesday, current projects on Thursday, fun on Friday, etc.). At the very least, determine a schedule that reminds you of appointments for piping up. Third-party platforms like

Hootsuite enable this kind of thing. It is also important to understand the persona, the personality of your key economic buyers. Do they want tons of detail and technical data? Or do they want quick information with a "straight to the bottom line" approach?

Best bosses, creators of engaging content

If you build it, we've long understood, they will come. No wonder boards are putting social media on their agendas, CEOs are calling for retreats to explore it, chief digital officers are agonizing over its particulars and executive committees are reviewing its metrics. Content is king in this realm, and the biggest issue for any company using social media — which should be every company — is finding and creating quality content to share on a regular basis. It's a tall order, to be sure, especially given the sheer volume of material that populates the online world and the ever-thinning slices of pie available for attracting consumer appetites. But it's not so tall that it should send you running in the other direction. Indeed, the challenge of finding your own way to stand out in the crowds should excite you.

A great example of success here is Dr. Alan Weiss, a global consulting guru. I like working with Alan, who is an expert in the consulting game. He is active on Twitter and LinkedIn, and generates a podcast and two daily blogs. Dr. Weiss is seemingly everywhere on social media. This "social presence," along with his "Monday Morning Memo," "Writing on the Wall," "Word of the Week" and "Mentor Newsletter" have helped make him the go-to for leadership training globally for the entrepreneurial consultant. He is booked months in advance and makes millions as a sole practitioner.

Social media taps into a company's biggest advocacy group: its employees. And it's a good thing. Company messaging is often considered more credible when it comes from actual people.

Here are some tips for pulling it off:

- When you're out there making your noise in the blogosphere or Twitterverse or wherever else, **consider your audience.** Remember, your readers include a cast of diverse characters: current clients, potential clients, current employees, future employees and so on. Run your considered content through this filter before hitting the "publish" button.

- The key is to **know your target clients' persona.** A persona is a way to summarize and impart information about people who have been observed or researched in some way. While a persona is depicted as a specific person, it's not a real individual. A persona is synthesized from observations of *many people*. Each persona represents a significant portion of real-world humans. The compacted result enables your social media plan to focus on a manageable and memorable "cast of characters" instead of focusing on thousands of individuals. Personas aid designers to create different designs for different kinds of people and to design for a specific somebody, rather than a generic everybody.

- **Look at what your competitors are posting.** Casting a glance around at your rivals offers a great jumping-off point for starting to cultivate your own voice. You don't want to copy the other guy, but if you see that a certain technique generates a bounce, brainstorm ways to apply it to your own efforts. Likewise, if competitors are receiving lots of engagement with certain topics, figure out how to share your company's unique perspective on the same things.

- **Listen to what folks are talking about in the office.** Could whatever's preoccupying your internal team be of interest to your external team as well?

- **Follow news threads on your industry,** and use them as fodder for injecting your own point of view on a public situation.
- **Share relevant posts from news organizations** and others to your own pages. By riding on the back of insightful things someone else has written, you confer some of that credibility on yourself.
- **Play into anniversaries, holidays,** internationally assigned "special days" etc. These popular and widely recognized events provide the perfect opportunity for you to plant your own flag.
- **Dress up dry text posts with photos and videos.** We live in a visual society, and people like to look at pretty pictures. Take care with the quality. Even if a stopper-by doesn't read your content, you can bet they'll make some assumptions about your business based on the graphics you use. By choosing visuals that express a point of view in a creative, dynamic fashion, you layer your value with your audience. Use hashtags to index Instagram photos to popular search terms on the site. Here's another big opportunity for separating yourself from the masses.
- Don't be afraid to **poke fun at yourself** with your posts. Everyone likes bloopers.
- **Develop your own personal style and voice.** Remember: there are no expectations of this forum, and you are your own boss. Create and post whatever you want. But be mindful of it all, both in terms of individual online postings and how everything hangs together as a whole.
- **Be authentic.** Include your name and, when appropriate, your company name and title. Consumers buy from people whom they know and trust, so go ahead and make some noise about who you are.
- **Be present.** It's not enough for companies to simply keep a few social media accounts. They need to be boisterous

and vocal and active with their presence there. That means regular updates to all the content, including the company profile. It also means being responsive to requests and questions. On average, a range of studies has concluded, customers expect response times of a few hours to a maximum of one day.

- **Refrain from comments that can be interpreted as slurs,** demeaning, inflammatory, etc.
- **Remember the concept of community.** It's amazing the number of businesses that blast their trumpets across social media, posting ads, offering advice and commenting willy-nilly, but all the while failing to connect with their peers. Your community needs to be a place where customers and users feel comfortable sharing, connecting and receiving help. If you can hire a dedicated community manager to look after this essential, do. Otherwise, task someone with monitoring and following up on the information that you post.
- **Don't forget the value-add.** Everybody wants to get something. In the social media landscape, that means advice, counsel, tips, takeaways. Be generous.

The arrival on our scene of social media, this groundbreaking and all-encompassing vehicle of communicating with one another, with its promise of widespread dissemination and creative expression, has changed our landscape forever. And for all the flak the medium takes for its time-wasting, productivity-impeding powers, it's undeniably a boon to all corners of the participating world, including businesses that a quarter century ago would've been pie-eyed over the idea that they might have such easy, massive reach at their fingertips.

Learn to use it mindfully, and you will never look back.

Chapter 10

The Mindfulness of Training and Development

"Anyone who stops learning is old, whether at twenty or eighty. Anyone who keeps learning stays young. The greatest thing in life is to keep your mind young."

— HENRY FORD

The day you turn off your brain and declare it full, no longer capable of augmenting its stores even one little bit, is the day you commit to a lesser future. Lifelong learning is a splendid thing, celebrated for its multitude of gifts, a considerable list that includes enduring mental agility, staved-off dementia and a more engaged existence. Whether formal, informal or incidental, undertaken for direct professional improvement or more general life rewards, a continued campaign of training and development is always a good idea.

This is especially so today, when technology is advancing at a pace rapid enough to light infernos beneath competitive sets and hike consumer expectations for quality and service to sky-high echelons. It's also increasingly critical to the world of human resources for the role it has to play in preparing workers for new jobs — no wonder Canada's Advisory Council on Economic Growth has recently urged a broader focus on lifelong learning.

And so it is that the business of finding and keeping talent is no longer considered the domain of the human resources department alone. Now it's recognized to be a large-scale strategic business priority; building lasting relationships with employees is very much tied up in training and development. Through the provision of learning opportunities, employees become empowered — and that sense of empowerment cultivates in them a sense of belonging and loyalty and usefulness. All good stuff.

The emergence of the millennial worker and the rise of the independent practitioner within large corporate environments underscores this development even more. **Now companies have to rethink their approach to talent and begin to prioritize the "individual."** In this new landscape, they must focus on a path of constant evolution, and provide a new mechanism for seeing that through — a learning model that can adapt to the needs of a changing workforce and align closely with organizational objectives.

Some of the best companies today have embraced this reality, and adopted a course of continuous learning and development as a key element to their organizational success. They may have hired professional trainers to conduct sessions on a range of topics designed to achieve success in the workplace, or assigned the oversight role to someone in their firm with a strong grasp of the training piece.

Renowned management-consultant guru Peter Drucker once declared that training and development would soon reign as the world's fastest-growing industry as the economy replaces industrial workers with knowledge workers. Details on the particulars of this grand transition abound, but one estimate predicts that technology is de-skilling 75 percent of the American population, a statistic that can fairly reasonably be extrapolated to represent the scene in developing nations worldwide, along with countries currently on the threshold of development. In Japan, for example, where women are increasingly joining the workforce in jobs traditionally filled by men, training is a mainstay (and not only to prepare them for the rigors of physically demanding jobs, but for facing such intangibles as sexual harassment and more socially oriented workplace expectations).

Because as much as encroaching and exploding technology is responsible for the world's increased need for corporate training and development, the latter is also critical for the individual development and progress of the employee — those elements of his on-the-job experience that motivate him to work for a particular organization over another. These are the spiritual, self-improving parts of the development pie — think effective communication, time management, active listening, even public speaking — that spur productivity and performance, and are arguably just as vital to an individual's experience on the job as her mastery of practical skill sets.

What are employee training and development?

Employee training and employee development are unique beasts, and not just for the more linguistically particular in our midst. Workplace training, at its most stripped down, is straight-up education for workers with a focus on improving their facility with specific tasks. Here's where staffers learn new computer programs and corporate protocols, material-handling details and operational procedures. Practical stuff.

Employee development, on the other hand, is the fuzzier world of improvement. What people learn under this umbrella is generally associated with employee-centric enhancement of more generalized skills and pursuits of well-being, always with a view to increasing performance. Workplace development is often seen through such channels as coaching and mentoring, self-paced activities, e-learning and modularization. It's typically delivered by way of a corporation-led program of ongoing learning in which — critically — the employee in its receipt plays a role in its dissemination.

As such, it is the individual's responsibility to commit to an evolved self, to identify goals and activities for development and to prepare a personalized plan that's as challenging as it is reasonably achieved. For its part, management is responsible for providing the resources and environment to support the growth and development needs of the individual employee.

Ideally, a company's training and development arms are aligned. That they're sometimes not might be behind statistics that show that between 50 and 80 percent of all learning and development activities are what's referred to as "scrap learning." Here is "learning" whose lessons are never actually applied on the job.

An employee training session may be a staff member's first return to the classroom since his high school or post-secondary days. For others, continuing education may be a regular part of their professional life. An effective trainer needs to consider both groups of individuals in his "classroom" and cater to each one's different needs — oftentimes inside the same teaching session. The distinction is important. The first group needs a certain ramping-up period; the latter can be approached from a more sophisticated starting point.

It goes without saying that some of your muscles are more developed than others. Maybe you're better at opening a sale, maybe you're better at closing. Do you set an agenda and map your world to the other guy's world, or do you just show up and go right into your presentation? Depending on your answer, you'll need different muscles primed. Enter the nuanced and customizable world of training and development. Across the board, the process of education has to be carefully calibrated according to the muscles people have and the muscles that require conditioning.

Getting started

It's smart to launch a corporate commitment to learning and development by way of the creation of an individual development plan. In other words, to have every employee set to writing a kind of pledge to transformation, complete with specifics like goals and timelines for achieving them. This document, produced cooperatively by employee and management, serves as a meaningful jumping-off point for each new stage of ongoing improvement. It's also a touchstone for checking in on progress in the stretch to come.

When crafting the plan, employees and management alike need to think in terms of writing up something that's attractive. In other words, the end product has to actually inspire the employee to want to put in a certain amount of effort. Start off by being specific about the *present*, so you give yourself something to work from. Here, managers should conduct a tally of every employee's existing skills, abilities, values, strengths and weaknesses. From there, they should nominate changes they wish to see in each column. The plan should be compelling, interesting, achievable, practical and realistic.

Next, the participants in a plan's creation need to assess an employee's current position and work environment. That means identifying the job requirements and performance expectations of the position as it exists today, along with the knowledge, skills and abilities that will enhance the individual's ability to perform it tomorrow. This is where you name goals and assign dates. Get specific.

The final piece of the puzzle is to set a plan and schedule for reviewing progress with a supervisor.

Making it personal

The attention to detail is key. Too many training programs in the North American workplace simply say, "Congratulations, you're going to be a CSR in the call center. Learn our script. Don't add any personality to it." You're increasingly seeing a revolt against this approach, and more and more service centers are now asking for personality to be included in the interactions. It is this point of individualization, after all, that allows for excellence. Every Christmas, my wife and I go to New York City for a holiday getaway. Four years ago, we were in a restaurant overlooking Central Park, and we saw a horse and buggy. It would be great, I told our waiter, if my wife could have a chance to go in one of those contraptions and tour the park in it. He took it upon himself to go and arrange it. He'd been trained that way, to be in tune with customers' individual needs.

That sensitivity to others' conditions finds ample application in training. In too many training programs, they're not mindful of the person they're training, not sensitive to the particular way that they learn. That's a ham-fisted approach. Everyone, after all, has a different runway to trainability. Some folks' cognitive agility means it takes them longer to gain new concepts. Others have a short takeoff and landing for obtaining new knowledge. I worked once with someone who took fourteen years to finish her PhD. That didn't make her a lesser intellect than the guy who did his in a year and a half — that's just the way she took on information. The worker who's slow to trust and prefers an analytical approach to taking on new information needs a mindful manager who mirrors these traits in the delivery of the training.

It takes one of our clients, Salesforce.com, twelve months to ramp up a new salesperson. If I hire someone and in twelve months and they still haven't got it, that's lost productivity that I can't get back. But if I hire someone with a six-month ramp-up, I've just gained six months in productivity. In some worlds — think construction, safety, transportation and power — companies overinvest in training because their critical applications call them to. They must spend a lot of time training supervisors about all of the lockdowns and protocols needed for powerline technicians and so on, because they know that if they cut any corners, an individual could suffer a life-threatening accident. They can't afford to deviate from the plan. It's when an assertive boss pushes their workers outside of their comfort and training zones that accidents happen. That's why the training plan in these scenarios has to be mapped in this very detailed, very sequential way.

Why is it important?

Everybody knows about the benefits of company investment in employee development. With it, everything increases: innovation, organizational agility, market share, efficiency, quality of work, employee retention, worker engagement. Only one significant thing decreases, and it's a doozy: the skills gap.

North America, it has long been reported, is on the brink of a significant skills gap. By 2019, the research predicted, there will be 182,000 robust, well-paying jobs in information and communications technology in Canada — think computer programmers, information systems analysts, software engineers — that will go unfilled because there simply won't be people qualified to occupy them. In 2016, according to a survey by the Canadian Internet Registration Authority, 40 percent of IT leaders had trouble finding IT pros with the right skills, and 46 percent said they'd struggled to fill their positions the previous year.

And a focus on training and development is important, too, for the culture with which it gifts a company. By making clear and particular its devotion to an ongoing campaign of employee improvement, an organization speaks volumes about its interest in the well-being of its workers. That kind of company is better, happier, more rewarding to work for than the one that's made no move to broaden its corporate knowledge base.

The Singapore example

Singapore offers an enlightening and in-action illustration of a nationwide dedication to training and development. Indeed, so remarkable is this city-state's devotion to staying sharp that a white paper published in July 2017 by the World Economic Forum (WEF) on accelerating re-skilling held it up as an example of how a country might get behind a skills push. A Lifelong Learning Endowment Fund focused on acquiring and promoting skills development was created in Singapore in 2001. And there's a slew of incentives besides, all aimed at promoting a course of enduring learning for citizens, including the creation of special institutions to train teachers specifically for adult re-skilling, and the SkillsFuture program. This sweeping initiative is aimed at providing Singaporean residents "with the opportunities to develop their fullest potential throughout life, regardless of their starting points."

A financial incentive — a US $500 tax credit, to start, topped up over the lifetime of a career — encourages "individual owner-ship of skills development and lifelong learning." This call to personal responsibility is important to seeing a learning initia-tive through.

These initiatives are undertaken in an environment of urgency. That same WEF white paper highlighted data from the Organisation for Economic Co-operation and Development that found that one in four adults reported a mismatch between the skills they possessed and the skills required for their jobs. Additionally, it noted, about 35 percent of skills demanded across industries will change by 2020. It also unearthed a worrying discrepancy between need and reality, finding that 63 percent of workers in the States reported some job-related training in the prior year — but this in spite of the fact that their employers simultaneously claimed to be laboring against talent shortages.

"A new deal for lifelong learning is needed globally to provide dynamic and inclusive lifelong learning systems to both resolve the immediate challenge and to create sustainable models for the future," the report concluded.

No question, a mindful commitment to lifelong learning, training and personal development that spans all levels of government and business is key.

Mindful workplace training

As with so many elements of her position heading up a crew of subordinates, a manager needs to act as a guiding force whose actions and attitudes influence everyone around her in the training-and-development enterprise. File here everything from sharpening focus and attention in the age of digital distraction to the power of pausing and navigating stress. And the most critical lesson a corporate boss teaches her underlings with her emphasis on ongoing training and development? That she cares about the subject at all. By making a commitment to personal evolution a priority, a manager enriches her employees with an inherent appreciation for its value.

More than that, a training-and-development program finds success in an environment that bears in mind the importance of how participants experience it. After all, as anyone who's ever been on a diet or a New Year's campaign of improved fitness can tell you, if you don't like the program, you won't stick with it. Herewith, some elemental characteristics of an employee training-and-development program that has the best chance of sticking:

- It unfolds in **an informal, safe and supportive environment** that always demonstrates respect for its participants.

- **Its goals are clear,** and based on a solid understanding of the knowledge, skills and abilities that the organization will need in the future.
- Its participants are involved in nominating the **knowledge, skills and abilities** of which they're in pursuit.
- It employs real-life examples in a practical and **problem-centered approach.**
- It draws **useful connections** between an employee's past learning and work experience with the new material being introduced.
- It looks for learning opportunities in **everyday activity.**
- It **supports staff** when they identify learning activities that make them an asset to the organization.
- The employees are given an opportunity to **reinforce what they learn** by practicing.
- The learning opportunity **promotes positive self-esteem.**

The learning options

Opportunities for professional training are plentiful today. From the IT guy running lunchtime boardroom sessions on mastering Excel to full-blown interactive-learning programs that train workers on Salesforce (for the thousands of jobs that are predicted to come looking for people skilled on this platform in the coming months and years), training and development can unfold anywhere and anytime.

MOOCs

Among the sexier and more affordable trends for information delivery for companies that don't want to invest the time or dollars in intensive formal education are the MOOCs, or Massive Open Online Courses. I took one this year from Columbia University in NY. It was delivered in short bursts, with video sessions and follow up work items. A neat process; however, you must be motivated and set aside the time diligently.

A concept that's been sweeping the education scene on the strength of its applicable novelty for the past few years, MOOCs first entered our educational conversations in 2008, but didn't attract a lot of attention until 2012, when Stanford University took its first kick at the MOOC can. Ever since, MOOCs have increased their stature as learning options for businesses, nudging the concept out of the realm of higher-education reform into corporate training — a $150-billion industry in the States. Massive Open Online Courses are widely believed to offer higher quality standards than traditional e-learning, at lower costs. Today, these online college-level classes — which are free and open to anyone — are on the offerings rosters of some of the world's most prestigious universities.

In this revolutionary model, the classroom is flipped. The majority of MOOC learning happens not with a professor lecturing students, but with students exploiting access to available course materials that they explore in the company of both fellow learners and the prof, whose physical presence is far from them.

Most of the educational interaction in a MOOC takes place in a virtual space, in web discussion groups with cohorts of learners, on wikis or via digital videos of flesh-and-blood professors giving lectures to a camera. Learners participate in student assessments and do online tests, quizzes and proctored exams. Upon completion, MOOC participants may receive a "verified certificate" or even a college credit.

Increasingly, HR managers are coming around to the value of MOOCs for the opportunity they offer employees for personalized learning paths designed to help them acquire very specific (and applicable) skills and competencies. Today, MOOCs are part of corporate e-learning's game-changing panorama.

On-the-job experience

I have seen leaders learn in many communities. I am a big fan of joining social committees either at work or in volunteer agencies. Many leaders I have worked with have taken volunteer committee experiences back to their day jobs, with dramatic success.

Conferences and forums can be wonderful ways to gain new insights, ideas and avenues for fresh revenue streams. Fight back not to just attend and get a suntan but also to circulate and "percolate," and learning will be enhanced.

Accepting new projects and taking on a job-expanding, job-rotation or job-shadowing role will allow the leader new insights and new stretch experiences — and learning is sure to follow also.

Classroom training

- Courses, seminars, workshops, update certifications ahead of time, seek new skills.
- Are you AI-certified in marketing yet?

Off-the-job learning

- Courses offered by colleges or universities.
- Professional associations.
- Reading groups (also called learning circles or reading circles).
- Self-study.

Learning and development programs: best practices

As with every other aspect of corporate excellence, it's wise to consider training and development programs inside a best-practice paradigm. And trainers, whether on staff, digital or helicoptered in to oversee this, need to be mindful of these best practices in order to get the most out of the exercise.

Consider that training programs should be

- **Strategy-driven and aligned with organizational objectives.** If the learning and development isn't in harmony with the organization's overall strategic goals, then they're adding a wrinkle to the corporate scene that distracts and diverts. Ideally, the training in which a corporation's workers engage interacts closely with the needs of the company's clients. That means identifying business objectives first and tailoring training in pursuit of them — and not the other way around.

- **Self-paced, and in touch with the needs of individual students.** We know from our work with our Cognitive Assessment Software from Predictive Index that each employee has their own speed to new knowledge. An appreciation that everyone learns according to different styles is a key component of a successful training program. A mindful manager would say, All right, can I use analytics to understand their pathway to learning? And am I going to make the investment to adapt to that? It may be practical, it may not be. Do I have the right people? Such sensitivity ensures success. From my

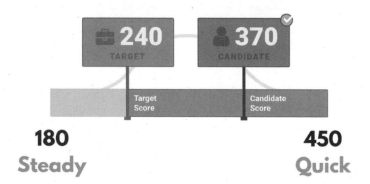

Source: the Predictive Index®, a registered trademark of Predictive Index LLC and used here with permission.

experience as a management consultant, I bring in the additional insights of predictive cognitive analytics. I rather like the Cognitive Assessment, which has its roots in a survey created and developed in Europe and formerly called the PLI, or Professional Learning Indicator.

- **Supported by key strategies, systems, structures, policies and practices.** Trainers should design learning programs that ensure that the education is tied in with and directly supported by organizational structures, lines of authority, decision-making, values and other business practices.
- **Delivered in granular, bite-sized nuggets of learning** that are embedded into the workflow. By making the opportunities for learning an organic part of a regular day, you increase the chances of the lessons being adopted.
- **Driven through multiple channels.** Think e-learning right through to old-fashioned classroom lectures — every approach has its pros and cons. By using a blend of delivery methods to suit learning preferences and learners' needs, the mindful trainer ensures that the training delivery method jives with the way each individual likes to learn.
- **Inclusive of opportunities to learn on the job.** Learning by doing is a massively successful means of taking new concepts on board — the action-trumps-theory argument in action. Some of the best programs see that through by way of self-directed training and development, wherein each employee, having ascertained his needs, creates his own learning plans and opportunities.
- **Considerate of the bigger picture.** That means consistently thinking about the root causes of performance issues and addressing individual situations appropriately.
- **Mindful of an agenda.** In this way, trainers and trainees alike are kept apprised of educational material and held accountable to its timeline.

Training best practices can vary depending upon a range of factors, including the culture and maturity of an organization. However, the best trainers make sure that they're up on training needs before implementing any initiative. The industry is built around the belief that the process of doing, reflecting and learning is a continuous one.

The future of training and development

Current statistics of corporate training and development paint a picture of a scene in transition. Brandon Hall Group, a long-lived human capital management research and advisory services organization based in Florida, published the "Learning and Development Benchmarking Study" report in 2014, highlighting key trends affecting the future of enterprise learning. It produced some interesting findings. Among them,

- one-third of companies are increasing their budget for learning and development;
- 41 percent of companies describe their culture as "controlling";
- only 10 percent of companies are leveraging mobile learning solutions;
- 59 percent of companies are leveraging social learning activities.

Although learning is among the most established areas of talent management, it is also among the most innovative. The flurry of recent technology advancements and rapid adoption of social collaboration have reinvented this world. That doesn't mean, however, that making a decision on learning and development is any easier than it ever was. Indeed, it could be argued that the enhancement of this scene has made locating a clear path for corporate educational improvement harder than ever.

Bearing those complications in mind, those with an eye on improving their lots have made endless predictions about what to expect in the world's next iterations of this corporate essential. Taken together, they recommend a redoubled commitment to a robust learning management program. Specifically, they suggest mindful attention to a handful of key trends and best practices that have emerged in the recent developments, such as,

- **Going mobile.** You can do everything on your phone today — why not learning? Still, companies have been slow to embrace mobile learning solutions (some stats suggest that only 10 percent are using mobile web-based learning solutions, 8 percent are using mobile learning apps, 5 percent mobile performance web-based sites and 4 percent mobile performance apps). It takes a little legwork to figure out your technology partner and your picks, but it's worth it. Everyone agrees that organizations looking to improve their learning functions will need to make mobile part of the equation.
- **Understanding social.** On one level, learning is an inherently social activity. Companies are quickly embracing social media and social collaboration tools to better engage employees and foster a learning culture. Although social has become mainstream, companies still lack the knowledge and insight around how to use these tools for learning and development. Companies, say those with a critical eye on the scene, aren't using all the social tools they might. While they're engaged in document sharing, discussion forms and blogs, they aren't generally using video or microblogs to improve their learning functions.
- **Considering adaptive learning.** Adaptive learning is a methodology that flies in the face of traditional models by inviting employees to learn at their own

pace and according to the most effective strategies for them. Staffers can be monitored individually and in real time to identify the most ideal learning approach. Younger generations breaking into the workforce with expectations for flexibility and work-life balance are well targeted for adaptive learning. It has also proven effective at improving efficiency, employee engagement and retention since it allows employees to build confidence and overall expertise.

- **Aligning with business objectives.** The learning of the past operated in silos where learning professionals had little interaction with, or input from, other areas of the business. The learning of the future will be closely aligned with overall corporate strategies and enriched by the input of business leaders to ensure that learning is driving everything from productivity and performance through engagement and retention.

- **Measuring effectiveness.** To determine the effectiveness of a learning strategy to drive business outcomes, companies need to find a way to measure it. That requires determining metrics — business and learning — in advance. Currently, most companies are considering team encouragement, employee engagement and employee satisfaction over such concrete business metrics as turnover, retention and individual employee revenue.

Chapter 11

The Mindfulness of Managing Millennials

"The people who work for you aren't building a company for you, they are building it for themselves — they are the center of their own universe. Just because you are the CEO doesn't mean they are coming to work every day to make you happy. They want to be happy and it's your job to keep them that way."

— BEN LERER, THRILLIST

For a long time, the collective consciousness was preoccupied with the baby boomers, that massive elephant that's inched its way through the snake over the last long stretch. But a new force has assumed focus. According to US Census Bureau statistics, more than eighty million millennials born between 1982 and 2000 are walking the streets today. (Definitions of the millennial generation — also called Generation Y, along with myriad other nicknames — vary, but most define the early 1980s as the beginning of the birth-year range.) That makes them the largest cohort in history. In Canada, more than 8.9 million people were born in that stretch.

At some point in 2016, millennials became the largest segment of the North American workforce. This generation is now more vital to the worldwide economy than any other. By 2025, they will make up three-quarters of the world's working population.

While it's important not to generalize too much (and the media have spilled buckets of ink doing just that over the last several years), there's no denying that the members of this generational cohort share a whole bunch of characteristics that distinguish them from the human tides who came before them, particularly in the workplace.

Millennials have been derided for a great long stretch. They've been blamed for defacing cultural institutions like marriage, devastating economies they don't participate in and upending business practices and hierarchies. They've been called entitled, self-absorbed, over-indulged, indolent and inattentive (their average attention span? twelve seconds). They've been accused of ruining the charitable impulse. They don't value money, allege their detractors, and are lacking in the patience required to climb the corporate ladder. The lax, permissive upbringing they've enjoyed means they lack respect for traditional structures of authority and don't respond well to rigid protocols or displays of power. They crave recognition and insist upon continual stroking. Leaders are smart to bring in the predictive world of analytics.

But critical appraisals notwithstanding, the sheer force of their numbers calls for corporate leaders to shape up and adapt their management styles if they hope to get the best from this significant and extraordinary crew of employees. Municipalities, organizations and corporate leaders across the continent need to know how they're going to recruit, train, retain and advance millennials as baby-boomer retirement accelerates. It's generally understood that brands and companies that can effectively manage millennials and meet their expectations will enjoy more success in the long run than those that insist on the old ways. That's why some of the world's biggest corporations have reworked their management strategies in order to make them more in line with millennials' tastes and expectations.

One thing I know about millennials — and our organization hires two or three of them straight out of school every year — is that they have to be managed from their world. More than the Gen-Xers or anyone else in the workforce, these folks demand to be treated uniquely, and by someone who cares. And while we're at it, they hate being called a generation. They like to be considered special, to always be learning, to have tons of information about their favorite subject: themselves. When I give a lecture to an MBA class at Queen's or Ryerson, it always strikes me that millennials are unlike other generations in their eagerness to have all the information there is about them. They're very loyal if they trust your vision, and if you're passionate about it as a leader.

When the leader parks his generational bias and brings in an evidence-based approach to people-communication with software like the Predictive Index, his staff often report back a more effective "he gets me" feel. The new insights from analytics can bridge the gap in generations. The analytics become a leverage point for motivations by real and personal drives rather than generational prejudices.

The millennial muster

Here's what we know about millennials — or at least what we *think* we know, since making declarations about a vast group of people is always a mug's game. According to the US Chamber of Commerce Federation, which produced a seminal report on millennials in 2012 — "The Millennial Generation Research Review" — millennials might well be the most studied generation to date.

According to this particular burst of research, some millennial tidbits:

For one, this generation, which has grown up in an endlessly wired and connected world, is extremely technically savvy. Eighty percent of them sleep with their cellphones next to their beds.

For another, they're considered optimistic. Forty-one percent of them are satisfied with the way things are going, compared with just 26 percent of those older than thirty. That's arguably remarkable, considering the troubles the world has endured over the last stretch, including terrorism, divisive politics, natural disasters and gun violence.

Still, nearly half of millennials consider themselves worse off than their parents.

When millennials were kids, their time was tightly scheduled by hovering moms and dads and abundantly rewarded by a system that decided *everything* was worthy of recognition. The prizes-just-for-participation trend was big for this crew.

Millennials are thought to be more tolerant of other races and groups than older generations (47 percent vs. 19 percent), with 45 percent agreeing with affirmative action to improve the position of minorities. Affirmative action, I am sure, has played a role here, and this is of course a wonderful trend. In the United States, this is one of the most ethnically diverse generations the world has seen for a long time. Sixty percent of eighteen-to-twenty-nine-year-olds are classified as non-Hispanic white (a record low), versus 70 percent for those thirty and older. Additionally, 11 percent of American millennials were born to at least one immigrant parent.

Millennials have been celebrated for their multitasking prowess, switching up among different activities without missing a beat. Some scientists have submitted this significant talent as proof that the human brain is evolving.

Millennials have a demonstrated interest in their communities and are very politically engaged. When our company works with charities that resonate with our younger workers, they seem to love it. For example, every November, our team at Predictive Success books an afternoon off and goes over to St. Vincent de Paul Society to prepare and cook a dinner for those who are at risk in our area. It has proven to be a wonderful team-building event that also gives back to our community, and it's the millennials at our company who get the biggest kick out of it.

The millennial group, however, suffers a reputation for being less concerned for others and with civic engagement (and more tuned in to extrinsic life goals) than those that came before. But it's certainly been my experience that this group is into its causes. We give a large percentage of our net profit to charities every year, and the millennial employees are great supporters of this. To my mind, they love giving back, and they're extremely generous in spirit.

The connection here that all leaders must realize is that millennials love a cause that appeals to their values. They will work for a cause they love instead of a job that pays 10 percent more. Map your employees in this area to a great cause in your community. It is fun, and it works. Recently at Predictive Success, our Shared Services team raised money through a Catholic charity in Nova Scotia to buy several goats for a family in Africa. The team loved this experience.

Detractors declare millennials to be consumed with themselves, a love they express freely and frequently on social media sites. The flip side: this is a confident, self-branding lot who are masters at self-expression.

Millennials' main sources for news are television (65 percent) and the internet (59 percent), both some distance ahead of newspapers (24 percent) and radio (18 percent).

Millennials' parents wield significant influence on their political views; in one study of young American leaders, 61 percent hailed parents as the most influential; public leaders (19 percent) and the media (12 percent) brought up the rear.

Health trends indicate that millennials could be the first generation in over a century to see their lifespan level off and even decline.

Rewriting work

Employment for a millennial is an entirely different ballgame than it was for their parents and grandparents. Here is a group that will trade off among a range of different jobs and even different careers over the course of their working lives. They're regarded as highly versatile in this regard. Absent for them is the convention of a single work engagement that draws them to the same place at the same time for all of their days. Indeed, the concept of keeping a job for the better part of your life is quaint and archaic to them. They have seen parents get "packaged off" after giving twenty to thirty years of their lives to companies. They know that the covenant with employers has changed dramatically in the last decade.

Reports on this topic by *Forbes* and recruitment consultancy Morgan McKinley declare that the average thirty-five-year-old will change jobs eight to ten times before she's forty-two and change careers six to eight times before she retires.

All generations have common traits, and common patterns tend to emerge over time. Would I call my three millennial children impatient? Yes, I would, actually. My son, Curtis, is a smart young leader. He has a JD and an MBA from Queen's University in Kingston, Ontario, and an undergrad degree from Eckerd College in St. Petersburg, Florida. He also believes he should be the next senior partner of the law firm that hired him two years ago. Many millennials were pampered by "helicopter parents," and they just expect more. A Workopolis study found that people who graduated university in 1992 worked an average of 3.2 jobs in the first twelve years of their career, remaining in each job for approximately forty-one months. At this pace, the average millennial will work fifteen jobs in their working career!

In contrast, a Statistics Canada study reports that two-thirds of Canadian baby boomers still at work past the age of fifty had at least twelve years of service with the same employer. In fact, more than half had worked for the same organization for twenty-plus years. In North America, we will have a gray tsunami, or a mass amount of baby boomers retiring. This generational shift is paced to impact the workforce over the next decade. On average, there will be 10,000 baby-boomer retirements in the US each day. This change will be the impetus of workforce planning globally for all organizations.

In 2014, the University of Guelph funded a study of a large group of employees in Greece. "A Comparative Study of Work Values between Generation X and Generation Y" is very helpful to understanding what company leaders will need to be hyper-aware of, and adds to a growing body of global data on millennials.

Using an adapted version of the Lyons Work Values Survey, the study showed that millennial-aged Greeks place more importance on the intrinsic and social aspects of work than on extrinsic and prestige values. The findings do not clearly support the notion of a "global youth generation," as young people in various countries hold different work-value priorities. This suggests that employers seeking to recruit, engage and retain young workers internationally must tailor their offerings to the specific cultural context.

The study also found that

- The oldest millennials had had an average of seven jobs by age thirty.
- By the same age, Gen-Xers had held four jobs.

Best boss leaders will be on a new path to not just hire but also "inspire" their teams. Employees have too much choice and will often leave if the work is not attached to their core personality and their "greater cause." The notion is dead that an individual will have a series of internal roles and move "up through the ranks" of one company over the course of a lifetime. The new-age leader knows that best boss leaders will help cultivate transferable skills with their employees on a new joint partnership, getting them ready for a host of roles as they move through the path of jobs in their careers.

The future is freelance

Call it the Age of the Gig Economy. The data — including a new study from Intuit Canada — pouring in about freelancers' increasing dominance of the North American workforce is overwhelming.

The Intuit report declares that, by 2020, close to half of working Canadians will be freelancers, independent contractors, contingent workers and so-called "on-demand staffers." At the close of this millennium's second decade, then, a remarkable 45 percent of the Canadian workforce will be made up of Uber drivers, Etsy crafters, freelance tax consultants and their similarly free-flying contemporaries.

The study, which Intuit undertook in partnership with Emergent Research, spent a bit of time exploring the forces behind this revised working landscape. It discovered that 47 percent of this self-employed population are going this route in pursuit of greater work-life flexibility — a biggie for millennials — and that 41 percent are looking to supplement their regular income. That traditional jobs are harder to come by and part-time work is increasingly the standard can't be overlooked either.

Hearteningly, the trend doesn't seem tied up in regret for old ways gone by: 44 percent report being financially better off since starting their self-employed work. South of the border, the scene's much the same. There, the Freelancers Union reports that fifty-four million Americans are currently working as freelancers — and that most of them made an active choice to do so.

What's more, the world's experiencing a growing sense of comfort with its revised professional reality. A survey by staffing firm Addison Group recently found that 88 percent of hiring managers are cooler with hiring contractors for senior-level positions than they were five years ago. According to FlexJobs — an online job board that specializes in freelance, remote and flexible-time work — some big-name companies are among the participants in the freelance takeover, including Facebook, IBM and BBC Worldwide.

Intuit Canada, the software organization behind TurboTax and QuickBooks, also found that 29 percent of this growing segment manually keeps track of their finances on paper. Keen to capitalize on this inefficient approach, the company has released new software for the contractor set.

Can't knock the hustle

The side eye had its day. The side boob, same. Now is the age of the side hustle.

It seems all the rage now, this concept of everybody needing to have a little something à la mode. GoDaddy just did a study and found that a full 50 percent of millennials have themselves some side hustle. More than that, their much-discussed demographic considers it the new norm in employment.

Author and entrepreneur Chris Guillebeau is an energetic advocate for this concept, which *Entrepreneur Magazine* defines as "a way to make some extra cash that allows flexibility to pursue what you're most interested in." The premise of Guillebeau's book, *Side Hustle: From Idea to Income in 27 Days,* is that almost anybody can turn an idea into a profitable side-hustle business venture if they're thoughtful, strategic and realistic.

Still, "side hustle" remains a bit of an amorphous term. The economically advantageous possibilities are wide open. But think here in terms of selling stuff online, walking dogs, making clothes, fixing stuff in your garage and so on.

In an article it published on the subject in the summer of 2017, *Forbes* offered these "three things you can do to identify your business idea":

- What are you good at that helps other people (Excel, career coaching, health, drawing)? Make a list.
- Which of these are people willing to pay for? Highlight or circle those choices in your list.
- After brainstorming ideas that you are good at and that people will pay for, create a statement that says: I help X people do Y so they can feel and/or do Z.

The GoDaddy study — which polled 1,000 millennials and 1,000 baby boomers — uncovered that extra income is the leading reason for having a side hustle (duh). And where millennials' side hustle often includes clothing and accessories, boomers' hustle typically involves consulting and tutoring.

Kayla Van Schyndel, CHRP, Example of Millennial Knowledge Worker

© Stan Behal

Kayla Van Schyndel is a millennial who works for People and Culture Lead at KOHO, a Toronto based software company servicing the finance industry.

She started her career with us at Predictive Success (only for 2.5 years . . . normal) as manager of shared services, a position that sees her responsible for a range of tasks, including HR-related duties, marketing, customer retention and event planning. Before starting with the company, she went to Brock University, in St. Catharines, Ontario, for business communications and completed a post-graduate degree in human resources management at Niagara College, in Ontario's Niagara region. She also took her CHRP exam and is certified as a human resources professional.

How do you think the millennial experience in the workforce is different from that of other generations?

I believe that millennials are changing the workplace for the better. Millennials seem to have higher expectations of their company/employer compared to older generations. We expect employers to invest in our development and to offer work-life balance and flexibility. People, especially those in the millennial generation, tend to job-hop, and employers have had to adapt to this newer trend. Employers are forced to care about issues such as employee engagement and job satisfaction if they have any hopes of keeping their millennial employees around.

How has the world mischaracterized millennials and the challenges of working with them?

Many people characterize millennials as being lazy. That's not the case. Millennials are always trying to streamline and find a better and faster way of doing something. We have grown up with technology and try to leverage it whenever possible.

What do you think are the principal traits of a millennial in the workplace?

We

- are open-minded;

- value transparency and having open and honest relationships with our managers and co-workers;
- consider career advancement very important — we want to have a clear plan of how our current job will help us in the future;
- are unwilling to sacrifice personal lives for work — we want work-life balance and flexibility.

What advice would you give managers around how to deal with millennials in their company?

As a manager, I try to refrain from managing millennials as a "group," because people are always unique and different. I am a big believer in using a tool like the Predictive Index Behavioral Assessment to help uncover someone's natural behavioral tendencies and manage to their preferences.

Thomas MacIntosh,
Example of Generation Z Knowledge Worker

Thomas MacIntosh is a student born in Generation Z who works for Predictive Success. He started there in April 2019 as a marketing intern and talent optimization specialist. Thomas is an undergraduate student at Carleton University, in Ottawa, where he studies international business, with a specialization in global marketing and trade.

How do you think the Generation Z experience in the workforce is different from that of other generations?

Gen-Zers put a large emphasis on workplace culture and co-worker relationships. It is important to us that the work we do and the values of the company we work for are aligned with our own. To this extent, we will seek out, and be more likely to stay as an active champion of a company who fit these characteristics.

How has the world mischaracterized Generation Z and the challenges of working with them?

A great deal of those in other generations have a false belief that all Gen-Zers are cellphone and social media addicted, and that this will render our communication skills useless in the workforce. Our social media and online communication tendencies are merely symptoms of our beliefs and values. Gen-Zers are collaboration-focused and value the larger community of the company they work for. They want to work face-to-face with others and see social media as a connection to the rest of the world, a way to extend collaboration beyond the walls of an office. Our verbal communication skills may be different than older generations, but our ability to reach beyond our company, and develop leads and business relationships online will create new opportunities for our companies.

What do you think are the principal traits of Generation Z in the workplace?

We

- are optimistic about the future;
- value companies and managers that are transparent and have a diverse social conscience;
- place more importance on what we do and the company we work for than on how much we make;
- want to engage with our managers and have one-on-one time with leaders who can aid in our self-development.

What advice would you give managers around how to deal with Generation Z in their company?
As a manager, I would focus on building a workplace culture that gives employees the ability to interact with each other, collaborate, and spend time that isn't solely work-focused. There will be a need for managers of the future to utilize team-focused data in tools like the Predictive Index System™ to aid themselves in hiring employees who won't just be competent in their jobs, but who will build a company culture and contribute positively to the team.

The retail piece

The sheer number of millennials out there means they wield a big, heavy buying-power stick. Millennials have significantly different values, beliefs and lifestyles from the baby-boomer generation. They have different shopping habits, preferences and resources. Retailers that acknowledge these critical distinctions, and target them effectively, will be rewarded with their business. And the worldwide economy will presumably become more robust in response. After all, American millennials have US$600 billion in spending power (projected to increase to US$1.4 trillion by 2020) in their vintage-jean pockets.

Commenting for a recent article in *Chain Store Age*, Les Berglass, CEO of executive retail research firm Berglass + Associates, said retailers keen to attract more of the millennial crowd would be wise to ask themselves: "How would I change my store and the messaging if nobody over thirty-five came in?"

At once terrifically misunderstood and patently simple, this cohort of young people is a box of potential just waiting to be unpacked.

The Cassandra Report, a long-established annual study of emerging trends, generational insights and youth behavior, took a look at what this consumer group is keen for on the retail front. More than anything, it found, young consumers aren't into overstimulating stores, and instead seek shopping environments and experiences that promote a sense of well-being.

Here are some highlights from 2015's "Cassandra Report: Body Mind Soul." Millennials

- prefer shopping in a physical store rather than online (as counterintuitive as that may seem), so they can touch and feel products;
- like the social element of shopping with friends;
- rank wellness as a high priority;
- desire balance of body, mind and soul;
- are interested in "a wholly focused, in-the-moment state of being";
- don't like loud, busy stores.

Given this (arguably surprising) reality, some tips for meeting millennials' retail requirements:

- This generation is suffering from some seriously strapped finances. They're awash in school debt and can't even imagine a robust savings account. Frugality and fiscal conservatism are good platforms upon which to reach them.
- Stores might strip down their on-display inventory to a well-curated, thoughtfully chosen selection. While they're at it, they might apply the same strategy to their store's decor.
- This generation is nuts for companies' demonstrated commitment to the environment, animals and green building practices. Stores that don't currently engage in such things should start — and make some noise about it.
- Stores should be decorated in peaceful colors. Rich hues and soft pastels like purples, light greens and blues fit the calming bill.

- Millennials are connected twenty-four seven and are delighted to use their mobile devices to shop. Still, research shows that most of them would prefer to visit a physical store (a recent study by Cushman & Wakefield says 75 percent of millennial purchases are made at brick-and-mortar stores). That means achieving a smart balance between the two.
- Retailers should relax their shoppers with ambient noise that soothes their soul. Think nature sounds or peaceful classical music.
- This generation is a tactile lot, fond of employing their senses in pursuit of purchases. The more opportunity they have to see, touch and interact with merchandise, the more satisfaction it gives them.
- Retailers shouldn't forget the value of appeasing millennials' sense of smell. Essential oils like chamomile, lavender and sandalwood are designed to help people achieve a sense of relaxation.
- The presumed brevity of millennials' attention spans is well known. Retailers can make a virtue of that with merchandising pieces that are bright, eye-catching and require just the flick of a glance to be appreciated. Also, they lose sight of fondness that this, the video-game generation, has for interactive opportunities at their peril. Shopkeepers should load up their stores with ways for them to connect.
- Millennials feel special, and so demand to be treated as such. They respond to efforts undertaken to give them personalized, unique experiences.
- Technology is king. Retailers need to research what's available to them and jump in with abandon. Writing in a recent omni-channel report, Matt Pillar, editor of *Retail Solutions Online*, noted that retailers are engaged in more of a "disorderly, staggered-start distance medley

relay" than a sprint when it comes to incorporating and integrating the right technology. Everyone needs to get on track.

- Millennials love to share (great experiences and bad; great buys and bad; great customer service and bad), and have their digital devices at the ready to do so. Brands that are cognizant of this will increase their chances of having good news make the rounds.
- Other businesses are starting to have walls that make for great selfies. Brooklyn bookstore Books Are Magic has a mural on the side of the store, and authors and shoppers alike tend to pose there and then post.
- This is a generation long accustomed to things being fast and easy for them. Shopping needs to meet the same bill. The stuff they saw online needs to be in ready supply at the store, and vice versa. And payment and coupon-cashing should be simple and mobile-friendly.
- Millennials are fans of digital everything. That includes snappy advertising and compelling in-store signage. Don't bore this group with static messaging. Stores might consider digital walls, like a company Facebook concept, and should maintain busy Instagram and Snapchat accounts.

The bottom line about this crew of selfie-taking, Snapchatting, hashtagging buyers is that connecting with them isn't the tall order it might initially appear. In fact, these folks are just as receptive to buying stuff as the wave of humanity that came before them — merchandisers just have to go after them a bit more mindfully.

Keeping your millennials

Professional millennials, it might surprise you to learn, are not particularly loyal to you and your company. A survey Deloitte published after surveying members of this demographic in twenty-nine countries discovered that they actually have plans to quit their current employer by 2020. What is up here? It is all around the point that all their life they have received tons of praise. Parents probably placed them in daycare, had someone else raise them during the day and then over-praised them for the few hours at the end of each day and on weekends. The kids were "over stimulated." They live in a world of very low unemployment, and when you add that they grew up in a world where employers were outsourcing, downsizing and resizing in record numbers, the old-style bond with employees has broken.

That's a crazy bit of news for a manager with an idea that his workforce will stick with him. Here's how that exec might turn the trend around:

- **Up the flexibility of the job.** This cohort has made lots of noise about wanting a career that works with their lives, rather than one they have to accommodate for. Baby-boomer bosses would be smart to acknowledge that desire and rearrange their focus accordingly.
- **Challenge them.** Millennials have short attention spans, a fact that's been repeated ad nauseam. (Of course they do! They've spent their lives clicking through zippy video games.) So managers need to embrace this news and figure out how they might offer similarly zippy challenges on the job. That means days filled with challenge, change and interaction. Ask them to step up to roles they might consider outside of their scope, like being mentors for other employees and in lunch-and-learn sessions that invite them to scare unique talents.
- **Promote them, early and often.** Millennials have got a bad rap for a lackadaisical approach to life, but in point of fact, they haul around a fair bit of ambition. They want to climb the corporate ladder,

and managers who don't let them destine themselves to forever be filling the rungs with newcomers. ("While pay is important, it's clear that millennials won't stay with companies for money alone," Deloitte's global chairman, David Cruickshank, was quoted as saying in *Fortune*'s "Why Millennials Have No Problem Quitting Their Jobs"). I see this with my three children. My eldest, Kelly Anne, is a consultant for Deloitte, and she has a master's degree and a strong record of success. She has enormous potential, and her company knows this. She experienced a couple of weak boss/leaders, and, smartly, the partners at Deloitte shuffled her around into new job areas and new projects. Deloitte spends more time than other consultant companies measuring and surveying its millennial employee group. From my experience, if you can keep the millennial past two years, your odds of keeping them to three years plus are hugely increased.

- **Map out a career path.** Millennials may be a bit bouncy with their employment records, bounding from job to job in a way that suggests a lack of staying power, but a recent study by Monster.com and GfK suggests otherwise. Here, 62 percent of millennial respondents said that it's possible to have a lasting career in today's workforce. Employers need to hear that faith and play in with a plan that facilitates it.

- **Give them stuff to play with.** There's no question that millennials were brought up in a digital frame of mind, and employers that celebrate that by keeping them current with the latest tech toys might get rewarded with joyful commitment.

At the end of the day, millennials are not nearly as flighty or frightening as they've been painted by the mainstream. They're just like their parents and grandparents in their ultimate drive for respect, engagement and autonomy. Give it to them — and get paid back in engagement, retention and loyalty.

Chapter 12

Best Boss/Leader Profiles in Action

We like to "eat our own dog food" at my company. We have wonderful clients across North America. We train hundreds of new leaders each year. Since we started in 2006, we have trained over 5,000 leaders, so we have a lot of data on what works and also what doesn't for a boss/leader. I have seen some very strong boss/leaders with teams of employees who would go through the wall for them. I have also seen some leaders I wouldn't want my worst enemy to work for. I have been amazed to see some boss/leaders with crappy offices and weaker product offerings create cultural-champion companies where fun and success blossom. The leader sets the tone, and great leaders can come from any sector.

In 2017, as we were researching for this book, our shared services team created a very cool national contest to study the personalities of the best boss/leaders. The research team — led by my daughter, Predictive Success employee Jennifer Lahey — offered a reward trip to Las Vegas for the best-boss winner and the employee who nominated them. Who was the best boss in Canada? What would their personality be like? What would their approach to being the boss be? Would they be in a fast-growing sector where hiring and money are easy and plentiful? Or would the best-boss winners come from a non-profit kumbaya atmosphere? The idea was to gather insights on who is truly a best boss and what type of leadership style they use to create this high level of success. Do they lead by caving in to their team, or do they lead by being hyper-assertive?

We surveyed our five-hundred-plus clients across North America. To help decide the finalists and winner, we selected a non-related advisory council who would read all submissions and report independently back to our Shared Services team. No members of the advisory council owned any shares in the contest companies, or have any business relationship with them in any way.

The leaders came from across North America, from companies ranging in size from 250 to 4,500 employees. Many of the stories the workers told were heartwarming tales that made it plain to the research team why people loved to come to work each day. Several nominees were not even aware that their employees had nominated them for this award.

My nomination: Randy Lenaghan

I nominated my former boss at Microsoft, Randy Lenaghan. Many of the lessons I learned from him are foundational principles I still practice today. Working for him was a life-changing experience.

The best leaders are acutely aware of the impact they have on people and recognize that leadership is about helping people become their very best. Leadership isn't a job. Leadership is a responsibility. Leadership is preparing your next generation of talent. It is getting the team to believe they can do anything. Successful leaders create a legacy. Randy hired more successful software executives across Canada than perhaps anyone else.

His former employees have gone on to success in Microsoft, SAP, Oracle, Bell, Salesforce.com and banking.

Randy was a "best boss." Best bosses are remembered ten years later. In one year-end leader survey, I said, "I would take two bullets for Randy." Most of his team thought the same. He had vision, had fun in everyday work and showcased our individual skills. We led the entire Microsoft world in financial services in revenue growth, President Club award winners and many best practices. Our team had ten times fewer employees than our competitor IBM's counterpart, but Randy's leadership was our beacon to beat IBM, and we did.

What made Randy extraordinary?

- **Randy had a vision.** He was future-directed and fun-directed. He could clearly articulate where we were going and how we were going to get there. His confidence and optimism about our future success was contagious. I would constantly leverage his vision as a source of inspiration for our sales organization. And guess what? His team were all "foxhole buddies," and we won. And won a lot.

- **Randy was present with presence.** He put in the work. He came with my team to executive briefings in Redmond, Washington. He supported us in relationship building: client presentations, office visits. He skillfully handled a supremely tough, often arrogant (now former) executive at Scotiabank. The leader was an ex-IBM account executive promoted by the bank to be a very senior SVP Operations in their IT centre in Toronto. His impact was felt daily throughout the organization, and he was always willing to give more, such as a phone call to an employee who made a big contribution. A handwritten note to welcome a new client. A lunch-and-learn with the team during an office visit. He cared about the culture of the company he was leading and worked tirelessly to continue making it our competitive advantage.

- **Randy put me in a position to succeed.** He wanted to understand how he could help me. He would work with me to eliminate barriers that might inhibit our success. He created opportunities to help me contribute more to the business. I felt empowered in my work (as did my team) and was afforded the autonomy to make my own meaningful contribution and imprint on the business. He was generous with recognition when it was warranted. There was an incredible sense of pride and belonging among our top performers.

- **He was invested in me.** He was a catalyst for my and my enterprise teams' continued learning and development as we serviced Scotiabank globally. What he couldn't offer, he encouraged me to seek out on my own. He was always interested in my future and made sure we were in alignment in support of my goals. He is one of the best listeners I have ever known — but he didn't stop there. He would follow up and follow through. He never made promises he didn't keep, and the conversations that led to commitment were always supported by action. Always.

- **He was my friend.** His investment in me went way beyond the office. He cared about me as a person and helped me understand that a life lived well was more about what happened outside of the office than what happened from nine to five. The friendship transcended business and served to reinforce my commitment to him as my EVP.

- **Randy would have fired me** (promoted me to customer who is fired) for underperformance. Our friendship (yes, we drank wine after work) never interfered with the obligation to the business. He was very clear in his performance expectations and candid in evaluating my contribution on a consistent basis. His clarity meant that I always knew exactly what was expected of me. If I couldn't deliver my sales number, he was obligated to find a sales executive with the talent to hit the performance target. That wasn't personal. That was the job, and I respected that deeply. Very few on his team ever missed their number.

- **He respected my opinion** even when it was different than his own. We didn't always align, and he was very open to my perspective. As I matured in my role, I would confidently express my opinion, and occasionally I could be aggressive in taking an opposing view on critical business decisions. I actually think he enjoyed the debate and defending his own position with conviction. It was also clear that he wanted my unequivocal support of key decisions, even if the decisions weren't consistent with my opinion (as long as they were consistent with my values).

- **He could admit when he was wrong.** His unique blend of confidence and humility brought him support in times of adversity and challenge. He made mistakes. We even had to put him to bed one time when he was enjoying a success party too much. He could admit when he was wrong. Being open about our missteps was critical to inviting more ideas and building a better business. Nobody was on the chopping block for making a mistake. We'd all make them and learn and grow together as a result. He was a true to his persuasive management PI report, a collaborative leader.

- **Randy was vested and all in.** He led by example and it was abundantly clear to everyone that the business was his life's work. His commitment to success was less about him and very much about creating something unique, special and sustainable for the people who were investing their time and talent into the organization. Yes, he wanted to win. I believe he wanted to win more in the service of others than for what it meant to him personally. His selfless approach to leadership earned an incredibly loyal following and is the primary reason I stayed with the organization for much longer than I had ever planned. I wanted to work for him. Others did also. He was a "desired destination boss."

My phone call offering my resignation was one of the toughest calls I ever made. He had class and asked me to work through the line manager, Dan Bloch, who was the future lead for financial services at Microsoft Canada. I wouldn't be where I am today without his contribution. Thank you, Randy Lenaghan.

Canada's Best Boss: The finalists

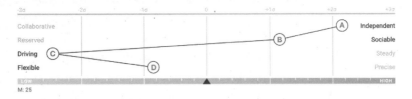

Source: the Predictive Index®, a registered trademark of Predictive Index LLC and used here with permission.

Tony Gareri was nominated by Olga Cenic. Tony maintains his position as one of Canada's Best Bosses by leading Roma Moulding as the CEO. Roma Moulding is a wholesale manufacturer of handmade Italian picture frames made from fine-quality real-wood materials. Tony is an assertive, tenacious second-generation leader who also "stops at the people door" with an authoritative but somewhat collaborative boss style. He has a sense of action and an interest in proactive change and does not need all the details before he "shoots the decision puck." Tony is a wonderful example of a leader who truly cares about his culture. He creates culture champions and is happy to share his passion for this on many social media sites with strong success. His company is growing well and he has taken a family business to the next level of success which can be extremely difficult. It is great to see that Tony has so much extra energy that he is becoming a well-known motivational speaker.

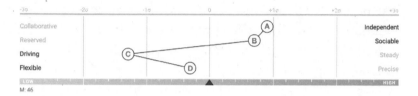

Source: the Predictive Index®, a registered trademark of Predictive Index LLC and used here with permission.

Dale Bauman as was nominated by Phil McQuillan. Dale is the vice president of sales at the Erb Group of Companies, which developed from a one-man company in 1959 to one that currently employs over 1,500 workers and owner-operators. Dale likes to set the direction. He also works through and with people. His preferred leadership style is proactive, fast-paced and action-oriented. Though his is perhaps not a romantic industry, Dale was able to recruit, maintain and coach millennials in a rural part of Ontario, and his "boss skills" were noted in very high Glassdoor ratings. He is a wonderful example of a self-aware leader who takes the time to learn about his candidates and employees, and who uses analytics to map their world to his. The end result: his people would drive a transport truck in a Canadian snowstorm to help Dale out. Erb Group of Companies is a fantastically growing company in refrigerated transportation across North America.

Canada's Best Boss: Lori Bacon

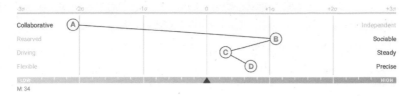

Source: the Predictive Index®, a registered trademark of Predictive Index LLC and used here with permission.

Lori Bacon, nominated by Leilani MacQuarrie, maintains her position as Canada's Best Boss as the president of Swimco. An altruistic-leader style. Not too assertive, very much a leader who leads from a place of conscientiousness. Lori is a collaborative, harmony-seeking, methodical leader with a high need for detail.

How Lori met Swimco

Founded in Canada from humble beginnings, Swimco has developed into a leader in Canada's retail landscape. Swimco was founded in 1975 by Corinne Forseth, Lori's mother, where it started as a mail-order business catering to competitive swimmers. Operating positively for four decades, it has since evolved into a retailer of twenty-five stores along with a strong online presence based on the principle that "We help everybody and every 'body' *Feel Good Half Naked!*"

After Lori completed her university degree, she started her journey with the Swimco team. Her mother was not only her first boss but also her role model. Recalling her experience, Lori describes Corinne's leadership style as supportive: Corinne believed in Lori's abilities and gave her responsibilities to show it. This support extended even further as Corinne allowed Lori to fail and learn from her mistakes in this first work experience, something that has proved to be invaluable.

Leading in the North American retail market

As Canada's Best Boss, Lori has continued to battle human-capital challenges in the competitive retail market. Facing an industry with a strong turnover trend, Lori and the Swimco team are striving to battle the skinny resume — a problem that often results in the hiring of inexperienced candidates. In order to combat this, Swimco incorporated the Predictive Index Behavioral Assessment as delivered by Predictive Success into their recruitment process to match the right candidate with the right job. As a result, Swimco has been able to find the best talent to help them achieve their corporate vision of growth and expansion.

Becoming Canada's Best Boss

Since joining the Swimco team, Lori has dedicated thirty-five years to leading others. Her experience and positive leading style earned her the title of Canada's Best Boss. The feedback from the Best Boss panel illustrates an exceptional connection between Lori's leadership style and the way her role model led her: "Lori has been able to create an environment where her employees feel supported. Lori makes sure to give her employees a sense of autonomy and ownership which allows employees to feel like they are making a significant contribution to the success of the company."

This connection is very special, as it displays the powerful impact of positive leadership. By leading others the way you want to be led, a positive ripple effect not only increases employee engagement, but it impacts the development of leaders within your organization. As Canada's Best Boss, Lori is a true testament to the power and impact that a great leader can have.

Conclusion

Many employees seek balance. They might be quietly aware that we all work for a third of our life. Unfortunately, we still see poor boss/leaders in North America, people who have never been trained to lead or be a boss. Many of us will have jobs we hate and bosses who are the opposite of inspiring. Today in North America, companies spend $15 billion each year on boss/leader and leadership development, and still we see that bad bosses are common in the American workforce.

Over half of our boss/leaders are not just bad but toxic at work

A study by Life Meets Work found that 56 percent of American workers claim their boss is mildly or highly toxic. A study by the American Psychological Association found that 75 percent of Americans say their boss is "the most stressful part of their workday." Imagine what this does to worker productivity, stress, absenteeism and illness in the workplace. If we could create a new climate where boss/leaders had real objective analytics for new insight into how to find the right employee and keep her inspired at work, engagement would soar, and we could create dramatic new levels of productivity in organizations all across North America. If there ever was a real business case to train leaders with a new level of insight, these two shocking statistics above are it.

A 2018 study by Gallup found that one in two employees have left a job "to get away from their manager at some point in their career." Gallup estimates that these managers cost the US economy $319 billion to $398 billion annually.

The study found that boss/leaders spend needless time and energy trying to fit square pegs into round holes. They need new insights, new predictive analytics, software like the Predictive Index to get objective insights for the multi-generational group of employees in today's workplace. It has never been more complicated to be the boss.

From my experience working with companies across North America, employers that choose managers based on the right skills and will (drive and behavior and cognitive agility, or what I will call "total talent") have a much greater chance of choosing high performers.

When companies get the frontline leader selection right, everything gets easier. Talented managers know how to develop and engage their employees. Our research and experience show that well-selected and trained leaders will create enthusiastic, "jazzed" teams that will focus on moving their company proactively onward, delighting their customers. The growth of yourself as a boss/leader and the growth of all your leader core will pay off in many predictable ways.

Companies and leaders receive a tremendous return on their investment when they objectively create fair and transparent job models for the leaders they need. Companies that create talent- and leader-based human-capital strategies that put more best boss/leaders in place will ultimately empower their organizations to leverage into their greatest potential — their employees. Having a job that you love and a boss who you like will certainly make the long 90,000-hour work journey much more predictable, memorable and enjoyable for all the participants.

I want you as a leader to get started with the use of predictive analytics. I hope this book has shown that analytics can truly bring new objective data that will transform your ability to diagnose, hire, and inspire a great team.

For each leader (and hopefully reader of this book), I am offering a free trial of Predictive Index. This very quick to complete predictive survey will help you first diagnose yourself in new ways and then, even more importantly, understand how to inspire the people on your team in new and insightful ways. For your free gift from me, contact my admin Julie Cane at jcane@predictivesuccess.com, www.predictivesuccess.com, or toll free at 1-855-430-9788 x 101.